Contents

Block 3
Products: New product development and sustainable design

Robin Roy

T307 Innovation: designing for a sustainable future

This publication forms part of an Open University course T307 *Innovation: designing for a sustainable future*. Details of this and other Open University courses can be obtained from the Student Registration and Enquiry Service, The Open University, PO Box 197, Milton Keynes, MK7 6BJ, United Kingdom: tel. +44 (0)870 300 60 90, email general-enquiries@open.ac.uk

Alternatively, you may visit the Open University website at http://www.open.ac.uk where you can learn more about the wide range of courses and packs offered at all levels by The Open University.

To purchase a selection of Open University course materials visit http://www.ouw.co.uk, or contact Open University Worldwide, Walton Hall, Milton Keynes MK7 6AA, United Kingdom for a brochure. tel. +44 (0)1908 858793; fax +44 (0)1908 858787; email ouw-customer-services@open.ac.uk

The Open University
Walton Hall, Milton Keynes
MK7 6AA

First published 2006. Second edition.

Edited and designed by the Open University.

Typeset in India by Alden Prepress Services, Chennai.

Printed and bound in the United Kingdom by Martins the Printers Ltd.

ISBN 978 1 8487 3052 6

2.1

Introduction

This block looks at the core of the innovation process, namely the development of an idea, concept or invention, or brief given to a designer or design team, into a new product for manufacture and sale.

This process is generally known to designers, engineers, managers and marketing people as new product development (NPD for short). While this is the term I'll be using in this block, you should be aware when studying in this field that there are no universally agreed terms. Other terms, such as product design and development, technical innovation, product innovation, and the product creation process, are often used interchangeably with new product development.

In Part 1, after introducing the spectrum of new products and innovations in Section 1, I discuss NPD at the individual project level in Section 2, at the company organisational level in Section 3, and at the strategic planning level in Section 4.

In Part 2 I focus on the development of new products (ecodesigns) that have a reduced impact on the natural environment in production, use or disposal. In Part 2 I also discuss the limitations of ecodesign in tackling major environmental problems, such as climate change, and hence the need to develop sustainable innovations that address such issues at the systems level.

Aims and learning outcomes

Aims

Block 3 aims:

1 To provide an understanding of the effective practice and management of new product development (NPD) as the core of the innovation process, during which an idea, invention, design concept, brief or market specification is converted into a product design ready for manufacture and introduction onto the market.

2 To give you knowledge of approaches and techniques for the development of new products (ecodesigns) that have reduced impacts on the natural environment.

3 To help you appreciate that ecodesigning at the product level is insufficient for tackling major environmental problems and that sustainable innovation at the systems level will be required.

Learning outcomes

As a result of studying this block and carrying out the associated exercises, you should have achieved the following learning outcomes.

1   Knowledge and understanding

You should be able to:

1.1 Understand the role of new product development (NPD) in the innovation process.

1.2 Explain the spectrum of technical change represented by new and improved products and product innovations.

1.3 Describe different models of NPD that focus on creative problem solving, design processes and business activities.

1.4 Understand how NPD projects in small, medium and large organisations may be organised and managed effectively.

1.5 Discuss how the requirements of the marketing and technical specification for a new product are taken into account in the NPD process.

1.6 Appreciate why designing products to reduce their environmental impacts has become increasingly important.

1. 7 Describe different approaches to designing for the environment: from single-issue green design, through life-cycle ecodesign, to systems-level sustainable innovation.

1.8 Understand different strategies and techniques for undertaking green design, life-cycle ecodesign, sustainable design and sustainable innovation.

1.9 Explain the limitations of green design and ecodesign approaches in tackling major environmental issues, such as climate change.

2 Cognitive skills

You should be able to:

2.1 Compare idealised approaches and models of new product development with real-world examples.

2.2 Identify technical and managerial factors likely to make a new product development project succeed or fail.

2.3 Critically analyse levels of environmental change in products, processes and systems that may help to achieve global sustainability.

3 Key skills

You should be able to:

3.1 Apply the knowledge and concepts in the block to your project work and, if relevant, to your work situation.

3.2 Organise (or know how to organise) a small group or team to work more effectively on a defined project.

3.3 Use computer software to help decision making in a technical or design project.

4 Practical and professional skills

You should be able to:

4.1 Know which important EU environmental and other regulations should be taken into account during new product development.

4.2 Use a materials database and life-cycle assessment software to help choose materials and manufacturing processes for a new product.

4.3 Conduct a simple environmental assessment of a product, or its materials and components, and suggest ecodesign improvements.

Part 1
New product development

What is a new product?

1.1 Definitions of innovation

New product development (NPD) is a term used to describe the creation of new products. The products could be anything from a chocolate bar to a hybrid petrol-electric fuelled car, and can include service products such as banking and insurance. In other words, NPD can cover a broad range of changes to the design and technology of products. In this block I'll consider mainly the NPD of products of medium size and complexity involving industrial design and engineering – for example, the development of garden equipment and washing machines, rather than chocolate bars or cars.

Before I look at the process of new product development, I'll consider what can be described as a new product. There are many classifications, some of which I'll review in this section. One classification you are probably familiar with from the *Invention and innovation* block of this course, refers to radical innovation and incremental innovation.

Using an example, explain what is meant by radical innovation and incremental innovation. Spend a few minutes on this question before looking at my answer.

Radical innovation involves a major new step in the development of technology. Radical innovations can have a widespread, and sometimes revolutionary, impact on individuals and society. For instance, the incandescent electric lamp might be said to be an example of a radical innovation that has had revolutionary effects. A radical innovation normally leads to the establishment of a new dominant design – a class of products possessing product architecture and features that have become the accepted market standard, and to which subsequent designs are compared. The effects of the electric lamp were only revolutionary once its technology had been embodied in the form of a dominant design (namely a filament enclosed in a pear-shaped glass vacuum bulb) and the electricity supply infrastructure was sufficiently developed for the innovation to be widely adopted.

Incremental innovation involves technical modifications or improvements to an existing product, process or system, such as the replacement in the electric lamp of the original carbonised bamboo with a metal filament.

The categories of radical and incremental innovation, however, represent only one dimension in the types of new product. This is because most products comprise a set of *components* arranged in a particular architecture or configuration. The components and/or their architecture can be changed.

Take, for example, an electric ceiling fan, such as that commonly used in many hot countries. It may be improved by changes to the electric motor or to the design of the fan blades or controls – these would count as incremental innovations. Or it may be replaced by a completely new method of keeping people cool, such as a ventilation system comprising wind-operated cowls on the roof that duct fresh air into a room. This might qualify as a radical innovation. But the ceiling fan might also be redesigned in the form of a portable electric fan with a table stand. This type of technical change has been called

architectural innovation

the technology of the components stays the same, but the configuration of the components is changed to produce a new design

modular innovation

the basic configuration of components remains the same, but one or more key components are changed

architectural innovation. Here, the basic technology of the main components (the electric motor, fan, controls, and so on) stays the same, but the arrangement or configuration of the components changes to produce a new design.

A fourth category is modular innovation, where the basic configuration of the components remains the same, but one or more key components change. In the fan example, a modular innovation might be a new design of portable fan with thermostatic controls and a tangential fan (with blades arranged like the paddles on a paddle steamer) instead of the usual design with propeller-like blades (Henderson and Clark, 1990, pp. 11–12).

In the *Invention and innovation* block you also learned that innovations could be sustaining or disruptive. A *sustaining innovation* improves the performance of an established class of product and hence sustains the companies and industries that produce that class of product. Alternatively, innovation may be *disruptive* and may displace, or even destroy, those existing companies and industries.

Disruptive innovations may at first perform less well than established products, but have other features that some customers value. Electric lighting was disruptive because, as the original radical innovation was improved incrementally, it led to a whole new industry based around the provision of electric lamps as well as systems for the delivery of electricity to homes and businesses. Electric lighting therefore largely displaced (disrupted) earlier forms of illumination – candles, oil lamps and gas lighting – and much of the industries that provided them.

Of course, not all new products count as innovations. Most new products, like the new chocolate bar or this year's model of car, are simply variants of existing products. One often-cited classification that includes both innovative and non-innovative new products is from a classic study by management consultants Booz-Allen and Hamilton (1982) (Figure 1). They identify classes for new products, including new-to-the-world products, new product lines, and additions to existing product lines.

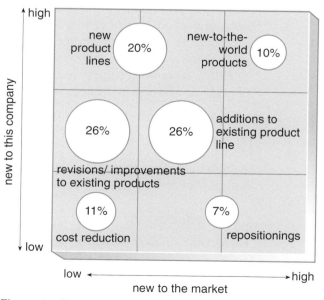

Figure 1 Categories of new products Source: Booz-Allen and Hamilton (1982) in Kotler 1988, p. 406

New-to-the-world products

These radical innovations are the first of their kind and create an entirely new market – for example, the original Xerox photocopier, James Dyson's first cyclonic vacuum cleaner, or the first home DVD recorders. They are only a minority of all new products – Booz-Allen and Hamilton's work suggests new-to-the-world products represent some 10 per cent of all new product launches.

New product lines

These new products allow a company to enter an established market for the first time. For example Canon was able to enter the plain paper copier market in 1968 when the company launched a range of copiers to compete with Xerox, the originators of the innovation. Most major domestic appliance manufacturers developed their own designs of bagless cyclonic and vacuum cleaners following the commercial success of James Dyson's cyclonic cleaner. Often this will require overcoming the patents held by the original innovator: Hoover, for instance, lost a patent dispute with Dyson when the company attempted to introduce its own cyclonic cleaner.

Additions to existing product lines

There are new products that supplement a company's established product range. Examples include the colour photocopier introduced by Canon in 1973 to add to its existing range of copiers, or Dyson's first cylinder cyclonic cleaner introduced to complement the original upright design.

Booz-Allen and Hamilton suggest that nearly half of new products fall into the above two product-line categories. Such new products generally involve architectural or modular innovation.

Improvements to existing products

Replacements for, or improvements to, existing products offer better performance, improved design, greater reliability, reduced costs, improved energy efficiency, or ease of recycling. For example photocopiers and ink-jet printers have received numerous modifications and with each revision performance, usability and reliability have been improved. Dyson has continuously improved its cyclonic cleaners with new features, colours and designs.

Improved products are thought to account for about a quarter of product launches. Such products may involve architectural or modular innovation and/or incremental innovation in the product's components or materials. But often they may merely involve minor stylistic or design changes.

Cost reductions

There are products that offer similar performance and benefits as existing products offered by a company, but with the advantage of a lower cost to the producer and/or price to the buyer. Cost reductions are estimated to account for over 10 per cent of product launches.

Such new products may involve innovation in the product's manufacturing processes, its architecture, and/or its components or materials.

Repositionings

This is where an existing product is targeted at a new market, market segment or application. An example is the repositioning and repackaging of the health drink Lucozade as a sports drink. Repositionings may account for some 7 per cent of new products. No invention or technical innovation is usually involved.

(adapted from Kotler, 1988, p. 406; and Cooper, 2001, pp. 14–15)

1.2 Spectrum of innovation

These different classifications indicate that there is a *spectrum* of new products from those based on revolutionary innovations to products that are just minor variants on existing designs. The spectrum spans revolutionary innovations such as the electric lamp and the microprocessor, and radical innovations such as the first digital cameras, to incremental innovations such as the use of microprocessor controls in many products, and design changes such as a new model of washing machine or mobile phone with cosmetic changes to the casing or controls.

This spectrum has been represented as an iceberg with the well-known but rare revolutionary and radical innovations at the surface, while hidden below is the vast majority of incremental, architectural and modular innovations, minor product improvements and design variants (Figure 2).

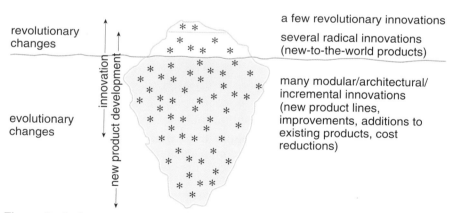

Figure 2   Iceberg of technical change Source: Open University, 2001a, p. 9

As this course is about innovation, I'll be concerned mainly with the development of new products in the middle and towards the upper part of the iceberg. It means I won't be considering what marketers sometimes mean when talking about 'new' products; the improvements, new models and variants of existing products that involve little if any technical change, such as the chocolate bar with a new packaging, name or mix of ingredients.

I'll also mainly be considering *individual* new products – for instance, a washing machine designed to minimise environmental impacts – rather than classes of new product such as fluorescent lighting or whole technical systems. Neither will I discuss many socio-technical innovations involving changes in both technology and organisation, such as the credit card system or telephone call centres – which have been called configurational innovations (Fleck, 1994). However, when discussing designing for the environment, as well considering changes at the product level, such as a greener washing machine, I'll consider a few such socio-technical, configurational innovations at the *systems* level; for example, a community laundry powered by renewable energy.

configurational innovation

a socio-technical innovation involving change in both technology and organisation

SAQ 1

In 2000 Black & Decker launched the Mouse sander (Figure 3a), a novel form of detail sander for the do-it yourself market. It was designed to have some of the qualities of a computer mouse – its small size to fit in the hand and the ease with which it moves across a surface – giving it the control to reach tight corners.

(a) What type of new product is the Mouse sander for Black & Decker?

(b) What type of innovation does the Mouse represent for the world?

(c) A new model Mouse with gel grips at the top and sides for greater comfort in use was launched in 2004 (Figure 3b). What type of change does this represent?

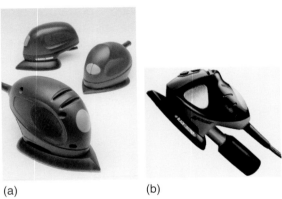

(a)   (b)

Figure 3   (a) Black & Decker Mouse detail sander. Clockwise from top: early, intermediate and final models. With each iteration the design became rounder, the cord tail was raised to meet European dust-extraction regulations and to reduce visual weight at the rear. It is marketed with the slogan 'every house should have a Mouse'. (b) Improved Black & Decker Mouse sander-polisher with gel grips at top and sides. Sources: (a) IDSA, 2001, p. 44; (b) Black & Decker

SAQ 2

Figure 4 shows a few of the over 1000 products chosen for the UK Design Council's Millennium Products programme. These products were selected for being innovative in one or more aspects, including challenging existing ideas, solving a key problem, opening up a new market, applying existing or new technology, and being environmentally responsible. So far as you are able, classify each according to the main type of new product or innovation it represents.

Figure 4 Millennium products representing various types of innovation
(a) Adaptive spectacles. The first spectacles to give the wearer vision correction
without the need for any eye test or the services of an ophthalmic professional.
Source: Adaptive Eyecare Limited
(b) Hi-fi loudspeaker. A loudspeaker that through design and technology
significantly increases performance over conventional loudspeakers. Source: B&W
Loudspeakers
(c) Electric violins, cellos and double basses. String instruments made from kevlar
and carbon fibre. They feature a unique active pickup system, producing unrivalled
sound and power. Source: Bridge Musical Instruments Limited
(d) Milk chocolate bar. The first mainstream product on sale nationally made from
fair-trade cocoa. The cocoa is produced by a Ghanian farmers' cooperative with
a share in the company. Source: The Day Chocolate Company
(e) Self-powered lantern. A fail-safe illumination device. It has wind-up and mains
charging units to provide light wherever you are. Source: Freeplay Energy Europe
Limited
(f) Portable computer and voice synthesiser for disabled users. A portable
combination of computer system, touch screen and voice synthesiser, providing
assistive technology. Source: Cambridge Adaptive Communication
(g) Solar hot water system. Solamax evacuated tubes generate hot water by
converting solar energy into heat, even in the unfavourable weather conditions of
north European countries. Source: Thermomax (GB) Limited

SAQ 3

Give two recent examples each of sustaining and disruptive innovations.

Key points of Section 1

- There is a spectrum of new products from a dominant design based on a revolutionary or radical innovation to minor cosmetic changes to existing designs.

- There are many classification schemes that attempt to encompass the spectrum. These include incremental, architectural and modular innovations, sustaining and disruptive innovations, new product lines, repositionings, and so on. But no single scheme can deal with the variety of new products and innovations that are created and introduced.

- This spectrum may be represented as an iceberg, with the rare revolutionary and radical innovations at the surface, while below is the vast majority of modular, architectural and incremental innovations, minor product improvements and design variants.

- This block will be mainly concerned with new products in the middle and towards the upper part of the iceberg, involving some degree of innovation in design, engineering and/or technology.

2 New product development processes

design brief

instruction to the designer from the client to take on a project, and background information for the problem or opportunity

So far I've said new product development is a process for converting ideas or a design brief into products. In this section I look at that process in more detail. I'll introduce a number of models that describe the NPD process in an idealised form and compare them with what happens in practice.

It is important for anyone involved in new product development to understand the NPD process. This is because innovation studies show that individuals, teams and organisations that undertake successful NPD projects generally do so in a manner that includes all the main elements of one or more of the idealised models.

Before I look at the NPD process, I'll describe how an NPD project may start.

2.1 Starting points for NPD

There are many sources that provide ideas, needs and opportunities for new products that may start an NPD project. I mentioned some sources of NPD in Section 1, and these and other sources were discussed in earlier blocks of the course.

From your study of the block (or the course) so far, list the sources that may lead to a new product development project.
Spend about 10 minutes on this question before looking at my answer below.

The sources of NPD you may have listed include:

- research, invention and creative design ideas (technology push)

- response to an identified problem, market need or opportunity (market pull)

- an order, brief or specification from a client or customer

- problems or deficiencies with, or ideas for improvements to, existing products

- adding to an existing product range

- market and user research studies, for example focus groups and user observation

- internal ideas from managers, research and development (R&D), design, marketing, sales or production staff

- external ideas from users, inventors, academics, scientists and consultants

- idea-generation workshops, for example brainstorming sessions involving internal and/or external people

- strategic studies of socio-technical and cultural trends, (such as those undertaken by Philips Design shown on the DVD videos)

- response to competitors' products, launched or planned

- joint development projects with other companies or organisations

- the availability of new technologies, components or materials, or changes in manufacturing or other facilities

- response to ethical issues, social or environmental problems
- legislation, regulations and standards, actual and anticipated, for example the EU Waste, Electrical and Electronic Equipment Directive.

2.2 Models of NPD

Whatever the source of NPD, there are many models that attempt to describe the processes involved.

Project level models are concerned with the stages and activities involved in the development of specific new products. *Organisational level* models are concerned with the people involved in NPD projects and how they may be best managed and coordinated (discussed in Section 3). *Strategic level models* are concerned with planning a portfolio of NPD projects that will support the business strategy of a company (discussed in Section 4).

In this section I'll discuss project level models. There are three main types.

1 *Creative problem-solving models*. These were developed in order to understand the creative thinking processes of individuals or groups. These models are of most relevance to an individual inventor or designer, or a product development team, when trying to come up with creative ideas for new products, components, or methods of manufacture.

2 *Design process models*. These identify the main steps or phases of an NPD project. Such models are useful to inventors, designers, engineers and project managers to structure their technical and design activities in a systematic way.

3 *Business activity models*. These identify the main business and marketing activities and financial checks involved in developing a new product. Such models can help company executives, marketers and project managers to integrate commercial objectives with technical and design activities in a systematic way. They are also useful to individual inventors, designers or development teams to ensure they consider commercial factors when developing a new product.

Figure 5 is a mind map of the different NPD models and how they are related. I will look first at creative problem-solving models.

2.2.1 Creative problem-solving models

In the *Invention and innovation* block you were introduced to a problem-solving model of an individual's creation of an invention and its subsequent development into a working product ready for the market. The model consists of five stages.

1 *Identification* of the problem – determination to tackle a particular problem.

2 *Exploration* – investigating the problem and the attempts at a solution.

3 *Incubation* – setting the problem aside, allowing subconscious thought.

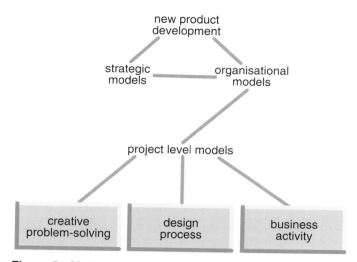

Figure 5 Models of new product development and their relationships

4   *Illumination* – an insight that produces a solution idea.

5   *Critical revision* – modification and development of the idea.

This five-stage model of invention, based on work by Usher (1954) and Lawson (1990), has some well-known historical examples to support it, such as James Watt suddenly getting his inspiration for a steam engine with a separate condensing cylinder while out walking, but much invention and creative design does not in fact fit this model. Most inventions do not seem to have resulted from a single major illumination (act of insight) following subconscious incubation of the problem in the mind of the inventor or designer. Rather, inventions and designs typically arise from deliberate and conscious attempts to solve a problem involving many small illuminations during this problem solving.

A more sophisticated model of creativity is that offered by Weisberg (1993), which is based on studies of works by famous inventors, scientists, artists, writers and musicians, from the Wright Brothers to Picasso. Weisberg argues that novel artefacts, including important inventions and artistic work, are not the outcome of a mysterious process involving genius or sudden illumination, but are really only the result of an experienced, skilled and motivated individual creating new arrangements of existing ideas, components, technologies, and so on.

constructive discontent

a critical attitude of looking at what exists to spot weaknesses and being determined to find ways of improving it

Weisberg sets out the key conditions for someone to produce highly creative work. A creative individual is someone who is *critical* of existing objects, including being self-critical of their own ideas. The individual exhibits constructive discontent – a term you may recall from the *Invention and innovation* block. Such individuals are highly *motivated* to produce something better and to overcome the inevitable difficulties in doing so. To produce a significant creative work, an inventor, designer or artist has to have, or to acquire, considerable *knowledge* and *skill*, often at least ten years' *experience* in relevant field(s) is required before it's possible to make a breakthrough. There are almost always *external influences*, such as using or observing relevant existing objects, which trigger new ideas. Often a close or *near analogy* (similar idea, object or principle) provides the idea underlying the invention or other creative work.

Case study   JCB backhoe excavator

Weisberg's model has been refined by Fowles (2004) and applied to the creation by Joe Bamford of the original JCB hydraulic backhoe excavator (the first of the long line of JCBs). Here is a highly condensed version of Fowles' account.

Bamford was an agricultural engineer from a family of agricultural engineers, so he had deep *knowledge and experience* of this field. In 1947 he designed and made agricultural tipping trailers raised by a simple mechanical screw jack. Bamford was dissatisfied with the load that could be tipped from his trailer – that is, he was *critical* of existing solutions or displayed constructive discontent. In fact, Bamford was well known for never being satisfied with his products and was highly *motivated* to improve them. So in 1948 he designed and built a trailer raised by a hydraulic ram that increased five-fold the load that could be tipped (Figure 6a).

(a)

(b)

(c)

Figure 6   (a) Joe Bamford's hydraulic tipping trailer 1948; (b) Joe Bamford's major loader 1949; (c) JCB Mark 1 backhoe excavator 1953
Source: J.C. Bamford

Bamford's idea for replacing the jack with a hydraulic ram came from his observation of hydraulic aircraft landing gear during the Second World War, an *external influence* informed by his engineering knowledge, and from the *near analogy* of the action of a screw jack and a hydraulic ram.

Again *dissatisfied*, now with the time it took to load his hydraulic trailer by hand, Bamford designed a loader comprising a farm tractor with a hydraulically operated bucket at the front (Figure 6b). Bamford perceived the *analogy* between the existing use of hydraulics for unloading and its application for loading a trailer. As before, his deep agricultural engineering *knowledge* and practical *skill* of fitting tractor accessories enabled him to put his ideas into practice.

The idea for the famous JCB backhoe loader arose as a result of seeing a cable-operated excavator on a sales trip to Norway – an *external influence.* Bamford saw the *analogy* between the cable-operated articulated arm and bucket of the excavator and the hydraulics and bucket of his loader. Why not put a hydraulic excavator on the back of a tractor loader? He bought a Norwegian excavator and spent much time digging ditches with it to deepen his knowledge of the handling characteristics and engineering requirements of excavators.

This enabled Bamford in 1953 to invent, design and build the world's first backhoe loader, the JCB Mark 1 (Figure 6c). The JCB backhoe loader became a highly successful innovation and since 1953 has been improved incrementally through numerous models and new designs (for example Figure 7). Many of these improvements have been as result of feedback from JCB buyers and drivers, which is a user-centred design approach as described in the *Markets* block.

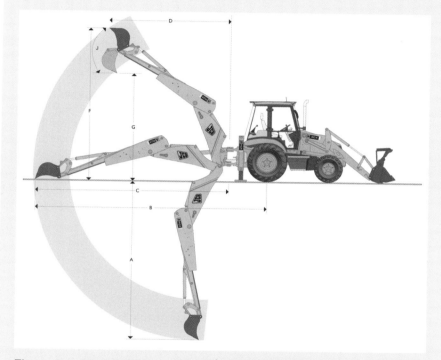

Figure 7   JCB 3CX Sitemaster backhoe loader, 2004 Source: JCB

The hydraulic excavator technology pioneered by Joe Bamford in the JCB series led to the virtual collapse of the industry that made traditional cable operated excavators (see Section 4 below).

Weisberg's model was developed to explain the production of major creative works that have had a big impact on the world. But the principles are the same for more everyday inventions and designs, although the knowledge, skill and motivation required of the creative individual or team may be less stringent.

On the T307 DVD you'll find videos about four everyday inventions produced by creative individuals – a non-tipping stepladder; a collapsible travel cot; an illuminated cycle tyre; and a better football boot. You should have already viewed these videos as part of your study of the *Invention and innovation* block. At a convenient point during your study of this section, view the videos again and attempt Exercise 1 below. The T211 DVD video about James Dyson's invention and development of the cyclone cleaner is also relevant; you may wish to view it at the same time.

Exercise 1   Innovation lessons

What general lessons about the processes of invention, design and innovation did you draw from the JCB and the DVD examples? How well does the process fit the creative problem-solving model of invention and design? Spend 5–10 minutes on this exercise.

Discussion

You may have noted the following.

- Creative people are dissatisfied with what exists and want to do something about it. They are always looking, and having ideas, for solving problems – they exhibit constructive discontent.

- A problem experienced personally or observed in others – tipping a loaded trailer, falling off a stepladder, nearly colliding with a cyclist, parents lugging cots in airports – often stimulates creative people to try to solve the problem with a better product.

- Ideas, inventions and designs for new products often arise and evolve through applying ideas and solutions from one field in another, for example applying hydraulics from aircraft to trailers. This is aided by access to a wide range of relevant knowledge based on experience, exposure to external influences and/or thinking in terms of near analogies.

- Producing a working prototype usually takes time. Sketching, drawing and/or physical modelling, and, often, obtaining money and expert help all require existing or acquired skills plus great motivation.

- Getting the invention onto the market as a new product usually takes even more time, help and motivation.

Success factors

The creative problem-solving model is mainly concerned with how significant inventions and novel designs are conceived by individuals and developed into innovations. It doesn't fully explain what makes those innovations successful, in commercial or other terms.

One crucial factor, as you've learned from the *Invention and innovation* and *Markets* blocks, is that successful innovations offer a significant relative advantage compared to existing products. This is crucial – simply being creative isn't enough. The original JCB, for instance, made digging in confined spaces much faster and easier, giving it a relative advantage over cable-operated excavators. But the JCB's success was as much due to the Joe Bamford's skills as a flamboyant salesman, who was able to promote his invention's unique selling point (USP). The continued success of the JCB business was largely due to the continuous improvement of the company's products in response to customer and user feedback.

The first three lessons in Exercise 1 are ones you may be experiencing in your own project work. Innovation, even at the early idea stages, can be frustrating, but can pay off amply in satisfaction and, sometimes, money. Take care to consider whether your idea offers a relative advantage or USP over existing products.

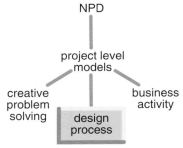

Figure 8

2.2.2 Design process models

I'll look now at design process models (Figure 8). These focus on the technical design and development activities in NPD, usually undertaken by an individual designer or by a design team working within a company.

A useful generic model is that developed by a British engineer, Stuart Pugh (1998) (Figure 9a). This shows NPD as a series of stages starting with the identification of a market need and finishing with a product on sale.

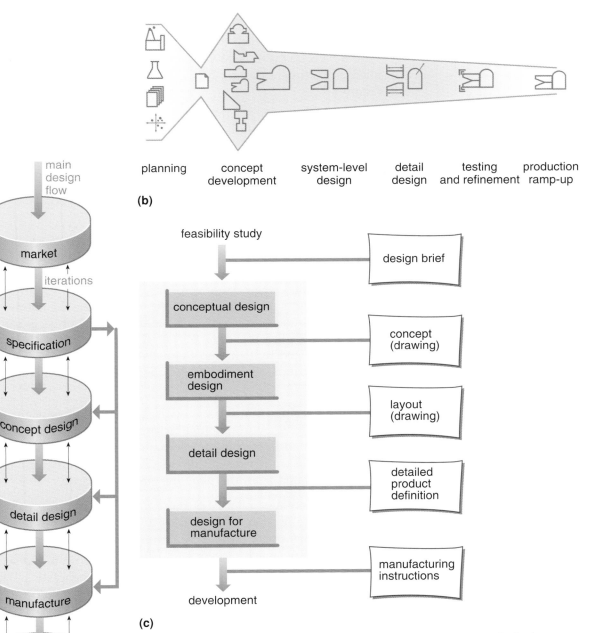

planning   concept development   system-level design   detail design   testing and refinement   production ramp-up

(b)

(a)

(c)

Figure 9 (a) Pugh's model of the total NPD process with the design core connected to the specification. (b) Massachusetts Institute of Technology's model of NPD. (c) Part of the initial BS 7000 model of the design and development core of NPD. The BS 7000 model has since been modified
Sources: (a) adapted from Pugh, 1998, pp. 6–7; (b) adapted from Ulrich and Eppinger, 2000, p. 16; (c) BSI, 1989 from Hollins and Hollins, 1991, p. 18

A similar model is provided by Ulrich and Eppinger (2000) from the Massachusetts Institute of Technology (Figure 9b). However, this model has two key differences. Firstly, it includes a preliminary strategic planning phase (discussed in Section 4 below). Planning then leads to a concept development phase that encompasses market and user research, specification and concept design (the first three steps in Pugh's model). Secondly, the detail design stage is preceded by a system-level design phase, in which the general architecture or layout of the product's main components is decided. You will recall that as most products are arrangements of components, this architectural phase is important.

A German model, which was adopted and modified for British Standard BS7000 (BSI, 1989), also includes an architectural phase, called embodiment design, between concept and detail design (Figure 9c).

The point of introducing these design process models of NPD is that although the names of the phases and the boundaries between each phase may differ, the models describe essentially the same process. They show NPD is an iterative process of first identifying a need or opportunity and converting this into a specification. The specification is embodied as an idea, invention or concept and then refined into a fully designed product that can be made and sold.

It is important, however, that you realise these models are based on *idealised* systematic approaches to engineering and product design and do not necessarily describe the more haphazard processes that so often occur in practice. Their value is to provide a framework any NPD project – including your project work – ideally should follow. In the UK many designers and companies manage NPD projects using Pugh's model or the British Standard BS7000 (BSI, 1989, 1997). The German model, originated by Pahl and Beitz (1984, p. 41), is widely used in continental Europe because it's also the basis for a German standard VDI 2221 (1987).

One thing missing from these models, which I'll introduce in Part 2 of this block, is how environmental factors may be taken into account. This has been addressed in an international standard ISO 14062 (2002) that provides a similar design process model with environmental aspects integrated from the planning phase onwards.

Given the essential similarity of these models, it doesn't really matter which one you use. So, I'll look now in a bit more detail at the design and development core of the NPD process. This is where product ideas, inventions, market needs or customer requirements are transformed into detailed instructions for manufacturing a new product. If you studied the level 2 *Design and designing* course, you may recall that this core comprises four broad phases (outlined here in Box 1).

Box 1   Design and development core of NPD

1   Specification

At this stage an idea or a design brief for a new product is elaborated from a set of broad objectives into a more detailed list of market and technical requirements. Identifying a specification for the product usually involves preliminary technical-feasibility studies and sometimes simple market research.

For example, if a designer or manufacturer of gardening tools sees an opportunity to develop a new form of hedge-cutter, in this phase it will be necessary to identify and explore the task or problem to be tackled, consider the potential market, the performance requirements, target costs, and so on. The integration of these market and technical requirements becomes part of the product design specification.

2   Concept design

At this stage alternative solution principles and design concepts for resolving the problem are generated and selected against the specification for further development. Typically, it will involve the production of sketches, drawings, 'lash-ups' or 'principle proving models' to test basic technical feasibility. For technically innovative designs, R&D work may be required at this stage.

Using our example of a new hedge-trimmer, a designer or manufacturer may consider different technical principles for cutting hedges – reciprocating knives, rotating cutters, rotating wire, a high-pressure water jet, freezing, etc. – and differing power sources, each one leading to a different product concept. The choice of concept depends on which best meets the performance, cost, manufacturing and marketing requirements of the specification.

3   Embodiment (system architecture) design

This is the stage at which one or more design concepts are translated into layout drawings, schematic drawings, mock-ups, visual models or prototypes for technical development and testing and for eliciting feedback from potential customers or users. They can provide useful indicators of market acceptability.

In our hedge-trimmer example, the embodiment design stage would involve deciding the architecture or configuration of the basic components (motor, cutter, shield, handle, controls, etc.), performing calculations and tests on cutting rates, safety issues, material considerations, etc. Again, these alternatives should be checked against the specification.

4   Detail design

At this stage the design selected at the embodiment stage is developed and optimised in detail. The final form and arrangement of components is defined, the materials are specified and the design is adapted to reduce anticipated manufacturing problems or costs. Companies with sophisticated computer-aided design (CAD) tools are able to modify the computer-based, virtual models made in the embodiment stage (see Section 3).

The product is given final technical and market testing and presented as a final production prototype. At this stage the drawings or models of the product specify every detail.

product design specification

statement that encompasses the problem, the technical requirements, the market, the costs and any environmental objectives

25

> For the hedge trimmer, detail design might involve analysis of strength in components or ensuring that these parts can be moulded, or otherwise shaped without difficulty. Test assemblies might be made using pre-production parts to highlight potential problems on the assembly line.
>
> (adapted from Open University, 2004a, pp. 107–8)

As I mentioned above, the actual product design and development process is usually less linear, messier and more iterative than the four phases in Box 1 suggest. There is often considerable overlap, blurring and feedback between the different phases, and other activities, such as production planning and component purchasing, frequently take place in parallel. In concurrent engineering, discussed in Section 3 below, such parallel working is vital to ensure materials and manufacturing choices are considered at an early stage of NPD.

The NPD process also may differ depending on whether the design and development work is done in-house or externally, for example the concept and embodiment phases may be carried out by an in-house design team or by an independent inventor, an external designer or design consultancy firm.

Choosing materials and manufacturing processes

As you may recall from the *Invention and innovation* block, the choice of materials and manufacturing processes are key elements of NPD. When developing a product, designers need to consider a range of materials properties, including:

- performance – behaviour of the material in the finished product

- processing – behaviour of the material during manufacture

- economic – the cost and availability of material

- aesthetic – such as appearance and texture

- environmental impacts – such as toxicity and recyclability.

Designers also need knowledge of a range of manufacturing processes. A number of different criteria can be applied to identify an optimum process: cost, cycle time, product quality, flexibility, materials utilisation and effects on the environment.

CES Selector on the T211 DVD is a comprehensive computer database of materials properties and manufacturing processes. You will be using it during your study of this block; it may also be useful for your project.

Design for manufacture and disassembly

As well as considering function, appearance and safety, designers should design products for ease of manufacture, to control costs and ensure quality. It includes, for example, designing parts that can be easily shaped using available processes, minimising the number of components to be assembled, specifying joining methods such as snap fits that facilitate assembly, using standard components across a product range, and so on.

Increasingly, as you will see in Part 2, it is necessary also to design products that can easily be disassembled at the end of life for component reuse and materials recycling. These are whole topics in themselves, which there isn't space to cover in this block. However, there are many texts on these subjects that provide useful guidelines, for example Boothroyd et al (2002) and Corbett (1991).

Standards and legislation

Standards, regulations and legislation also have to be considered during NPD. In Part 2 you'll learn how environmental legislation is having a growing effect on product planning and design decisions. However, many other standards, regulations and legislation may have to be complied with. For example, the prototype Black & Decker Mouse sander had to be modified to meet European dust-extraction regulations (Figure 3a) and European and US standards on the safety of lawnmowers and hedge-trimmers specify that the design must adequately protect users from injury by the product's moving blades.

I'll next consider two specific cases of NPD, to see how the design process models compare with practice.

After the case study there is an exercise for you to do, which you may wish to look at first.

Case study | Garden Groom

A retired British engineer, Graham Wilson, had an idea for a new type of hedge-trimmer that would automatically collect the trimmings. Therefore the user would not have the task of raking and collecting the clippings when trimming hedges and shrubs. He believed there would be a market for such a product and invested his early retirement pay-out and remortgaged his house to develop this new garden tool.

Jonathan Ward takes up the story:

> Graham Wilson's concept was to replace the conventional reciprocating blades with a rotating blade, backed by a helical screw device that would pull the clippings into a collection box. A second advantage of the rotary mechanism was that it allowed the entire cutting mechanism to be placed inside a protective cowl, making the trimmer much safer to use – an important advantage since hedge trimmers cause numerous accidents every year in the UK. Indeed the potential safety advantages of the new design were so compelling that the device's inventor was able to get two DTI [the UK's Department of Trade and Industry] awards for further development of the product on the strength of its potential safety benefits.

> At the beginning of 2001 he approached DCA [a major design consultancy firm DCA Design International] with a crude prototype built using the motor of an electric drill [Figure 10a]. The prototype worked well enough to demonstrate the concept, but it was noisy and uncomfortable to use for long periods, as its design required the weight of the motor to be held at arm's length during the cutting process, putting great strain on the arms.

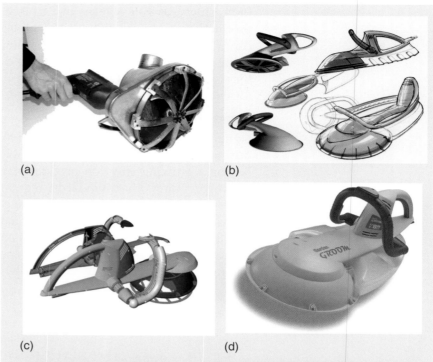

(a)

(b)

(c)

(d)

Figure 10 Some stages in the design and development of the Garden Groom: (a) initial test rig (principle proving model); (b) preliminary concept sketches; (c) 3D computer-aided design model; (d) finished product Source: Ward, 2002, p. 73

DCA's first involvement in the design process, according to designer Mark Fernandes, was a very traditional manual prototyping phase involving the production of weighted foam models to get the ergonomics of the machine right, followed by a series of physical prototypes of the blades to perfect the cutting process. 'It was vital to get the blade configuration right, since for the clipping collection system to work, the trimmings need to be cut as finely as possible', explains Fernandes. 'At the same time we wanted to minimise production costs, which meant that the rotating blade had to be a simple shape that could be easily blanked out of steel, while the static blade was shaped to optimise the cutting action.'

Other aspects of the design were also selected at this stage, such as a safety handle configuration, which ensures that the trimmer can only operate when both the user's hands are holding the handle at the same time.

[...] Three months of physical prototype work led to an optimised configuration that positioned heavy components – like the motor – as close to the hands as possible, but which still retained the full advantage of the novel cutting and clipping collection system, most of which could be moulded in lightweight plastics to minimise weight. A working prototype was built in part from hedge trimmer components and the second phase of the design process was ready to begin.

Fernandes and his colleagues then set about turning their concept sketches [for a full production trimmer Figure 10b] into fully detailed CAD models. [...]

The CAD models [Figure 10c] were built in two months, during which the designers also had to identify and find a source for all the standard parts, such as the motor, which were to be used in the finished product. The concurrent nature of this part of the process meant that the model had to allow for the possibility of late stage design changes.

As well as using a core Solidworks package to build the model, DCA also took advantage of a range of partner [CAD] products to carry out analysis and optimise the design, including ... analysis to prove that the finished components could be manufactured successfully and ... to demonstrate that sufficient strength had been designed in.

With the CAD models complete, the data was used to produce prototype parts directly using ... rapid prototyping. These parts, in turn, were used as masters for the production of five fully functional, polyurethane prototypes (simulating the eventual production material which is to be glass filled polypropylene).

The prototypes ... were ready in time for the GLEE [International Gardening and Leisure] exhibition in Birmingham in September 2001, at which [market reactions were tested] and the Garden Groom won the 'best new product in show' award.

(Adapted from Ward, 2002, pp. 72–3)

Some two years later in early 2004 this innovative product was in production in the Far East and marketed by a new UK-based business Garden Groom Ltd at around £100 (Figure 10d). A Consumers' Association user trial of the Garden Groom concluded it was an 'interesting innovation' that was 'worth considering'. It was slower than conventional hedge-trimmers and awkward for trimming the sides of hedges, but safe, good for the top of hedges and collected the waste trimmings, although the collecting box had to be emptied frequently (*Which?*, May 2004, p. 50).

As you saw in the *Markets* block, this kind of user feedback is often used by the designer or manufacturer to improve the product. A separate bag was designed for collecting the Garden Groom's trimmings. Continuous improvement, as I noted earlier, is one of the key characteristics of successful products.

Exercise 2   Garden Groom – theory and practice

Look back over the four-phase model of design and development outlined in Box 1 and the Garden Groom case study. Identify some of the similarities and differences between the idealised model and the real-world example of the invention, design and development of the Garden Groom. Spend about 15 minutes on this exercise before looking at the discussion below.

Discussion

Specification and concept design

Because the initial phases of product development were undertaken by Graham Wilson as an independent engineer, the processes of product specification followed by exploration of alternative concept designs for the hedge trimmer were probably not carried out formally or systematically. These initial stages were more a matter of individual creativity (as described in the

Invention and innovation block or in Weisberg's creative problem-solving model) than systematic design. Notice the concept's potentially greater convenience and safety would give a new product based on it an advantage over conventional hedge-trimmers.

Embodiment and detail design

The design and development process proper starts when DCA design consultants were given the task of converting Graham Wilson's crude prototype into an attractive, safe, economic to manufacture and saleable product. Such performance, cost, materials, manufacturing and marketing requirements are typical of most new products and should have been set down in a product design specification.

These embodiment and detail design phases of the NPD process match the idealised model fairly closely. For example, the embodiment design phase involved the design and construction of technical and visual models and prototypes to improve the cutting action and ergonomics of the product, and the detail design phase involved the use of sophisticated CAD systems to analyse and optimise the design, for example for strength, ease and cost of manufacture. Notice the choice of polyurethane as the material for the prototypes, which has similar characteristics to the glass-filled polypropylene used in the final production design.

However, market responses to the product appear – at least from this account – only to have been obtained at the final prototype stage, after considerable investments must have been made in development. This project hence involved considerable risk. As the *Markets* block showed, while it is difficult to get realistic responses to an innovative product, consumer testing at the concept stage can provide some guidance on likely market acceptance.

I will look now at another innovative product, whose development follows the idealised design process model more closely. I'll focus on the activities involved in converting an idea into a working prototype that satisfies a product design specification.

Case study   The electric doughnut

In 2001 a student designer, Justin Floyd, developed a portable kinetic mobile phone charger (the electric doughnut) as a final year postgraduate project. The idea came to him while travelling by train when he thought the swaying of the train might be converted into energy for charging mobile phones.

Market

Before starting to design, Floyd conducted some basic market research to identify the potential demand, and user requirements, for his idea of a mobile phone charger powered by human movement. For example, he conducted an internet and patent search for technical and market literature on mobile phones and portable chargers; devised a questionnaire for potential users of his charger; and conducted a telephone interview with a mobile phone manufacturer.

His questionnaire, completed by 33 friends and company employees, revealed that many people failed to charge their phones at night and were often annoyed by having a low or flat phone battery. Although he found over half of his respondents would be irritated by having to carry a separate kinetic charger, the potential market for such a product was large and so he decided to go ahead.

Specification

Floyd next drew up a list of 'critical success factors' based on his user research: for example, the product must minimally burden the user; and be seen as a stylish and fashionable mobile phone accessory. Some initial ideas arising from this design brief included a charger built into clothing or the phone's carrying case.

After carrying out some initial technical investigations into batteries and devices, Floyd was able to convert his brief into a detailed product design specification. The specification included both technical design, and user and market elements, such as:

- the product will use motion generated by the user to generate electrical charge

- the product will double a NiMH battery's standby time, outputting 30 mA when in motion

- the product should be minimal in size and weight (200–300 g)

- uncomplicated, simple and functional styling will give the product broad appeal

- where possible, the choice of materials and components will take account of recycling and other environmental aspects.

The process of design and development was then concerned with how to create a product that best satisfied the requirements of the specification.

Concept design

Floyd considered several technologies that might be used to generate electric charge in a portable device – a pendulum system like that used on some Seiko watches, piezoelectric materials that generate electricity by compression, and solar cells. He chose magnetic-induction technology (as used in a human-powered torch) as the starting point for his concept.

He produced his first concept design, a linear magnetic-induction device that would generate electricity when shaken back and forth (Figure 11a), and made a simple prototype to test the idea. This prototype worked reasonably well, so Floyd designed a second concept, a pendulum device he thought would capture the motion of the user's body more effectively (Figure 11b). He then realised that a simpler and better arrangement would be to have a spherical magnet running in a circular tube surrounded by coils. This idea provided the basic concept design for the electric doughnut kinetic charger (Figure 11c).

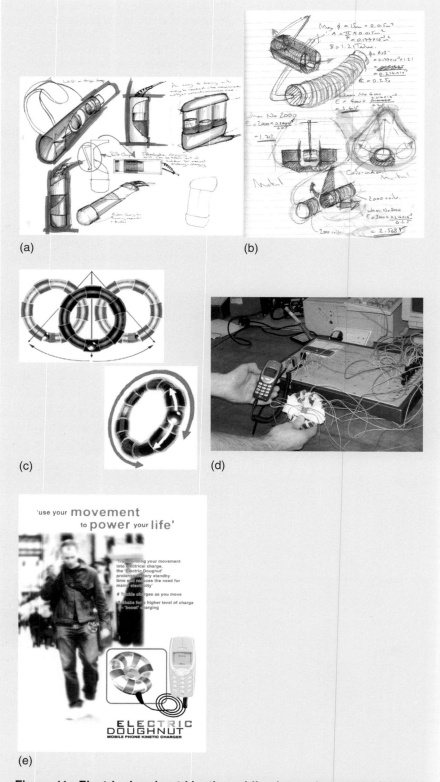

Figure 11 Electric doughnut kinetic mobile phone charger: (a) initial concept linear magnetic induction charger (abandoned); (b) second concept pendulum-shaped magnetic induction charger that led to the doughnut shaped charger; (c) third concept doughnut-shaped magnetic induction charger with spherical magnet; (d) testing prototype electric doughnut; (e) mock-up of advertisement showing chosen embodiment design for the electric doughnut Sources: (a–e) Floyd, 2001, pp. 32, 42, 44, 75, 99

Embodiment design

Once the technical concept had been decided, the next step was to produce a design that actually worked and met the user and market requirements of the specification. This meant designing a device that would be small and light enough to be carried easily and look attractive and fashionable. Again, Floyd created several alternative designs embodying the electric doughnut concept, such as a charger worn like a bracelet, a combined phone and charger unit, and a separate doughnut-shaped device. To help decide which embodiment to develop Floyd asked 30 potential users for their preferences: the majority chose a separate device connected to the phone by a wire.

Detail design

Floyd then had to translate his chosen embodiment into a detailed design that met his specification, answering such questions as how many coils of wire would be needed to generate sufficient current; what size should the doughnut be; what circuits would be needed to rectify the current from the device; and from what materials are the components to be manufactured? This required both calculations and technical testing using experimental models and prototypes (Figure 11d), which required assistance from a specialist electrical firm.

Costing

Having designed a working prototype, it was necessary to build it using realistic materials and components, to consider how the product might be manufactured, how much it would cost to manufacture, and whether this would enable the product to be sold at a price the market would accept. The prototype cost around £50 to make. With his knowledge of materials and manufacturing processes – for example using injection-moulded polypropylene for the doughnut core and casing – Floyd estimated his product could be manufactured in volume at about £5 per unit and sold for his target price of about £30.

Sales

Unfortunately, Floyd's prototype wasn't developed into a production design, or manufactured and marketed. After all, it was only the result of a student project. However, Floyd did consider the 4Ps of the marketing mix for his target market: fashion-aware teenagers, and 25–35 year olds leading busy lives.

Floyd's 4Ps were as follows:

- the *product* should be simple and reliable, probably produced via an alliance with a mobile handset manufacturer and with the potential for diversification into chargers for other portable electronic products

- considering the prices of other mobile accessories, its *price* should be £30–£40

- it should be available in *places* where mobile phones are bought

- *promotion* should initially be by word of mouth plus in-store promotion and, when finances permit, advertising (Figure 11e).

In retrospect, it may be argued that Floyd failed to spot a key issue at the beginning of his project. Once he had his basic idea of using the motion of the user's body to generate electricity and included this in his specification, apart from brief consideration of solar cells built into the user's clothing, he didn't consider other technologies that could have led him to a simpler and cheaper product. One such technology is a human-powered generator, as used in existing portable phone chargers costing from under £10 to £35 (Figure 12) and in a concept design for a mobile phone with a built-in hand-powered generator (Figure 52b).

Floyd might, of course, have rejected such ideas because they were not novel, but this case provides a useful lesson about not fixing on a single solution idea too early. Sometimes it's necessary to abandon an attractive new idea and select an established technology. Even if the technology is not new, the embodiment of it in a design can be novel and marketable.

Figure 12 Porta-Charge wind-up mobile phone charger, price £9. Three minutes of winding gives 2 to 8 minutes talk time or 30 to 60 minutes standby. Source: Porta-Charge Ltd

There's a short video about the invention and development of the electric doughnut mobile phone charger on the T211 DVD. View it at any time during your study of this section.

There are several other video case studies on the T211 DVD that illustrate the design processes involved in NPD. Optionally view any of these if you have time.

The T211 DVD also includes the CES Selector database. If you've installed this software, find the material Polypropylene [PP]. With the Table menu set to MaterialUniverse and the Subset menu set to Edu Level 2, go to Polymer > Thermoplastic > Polypropylene [PP]. Look at the information for this material.

Now find injection moulding. With the Table menu set to ProcessUniverse and the Subset menu set to Edu Level 2 Shaping, go to SHAPING > Moulding > Injection Moulding. Look at the information for this process.

Why, at the detail design stage, did Justin Floyd propose this material and manufacturing process for the core and casing of the electric doughnut?

Floyd presumably proposed polypropylene because it is a widely used, low cost, recyclable material with good electrical insulating properties. He probably proposed injection moulding as a process for making large volumes of plastics components at low unit cost, despite the high initial tooling cost involved in making the mould.

Success factors

What do the above design process models and case studies tell us about what makes an NPD project likely to succeed or fail?

- Successful NPD projects are likely to be those that follow one of the standard design process models, with feedback loops between phases.

- A detailed product design specification should be drawn up *before* beginning to design. This market and technical specification should elaborate the design brief (if any) and be based on research into user, market and performance requirements.

- It is important to consider alternative ideas and technical concepts to provide the essential function of a new product before deciding which to develop in more detail.

- It is important to choose and develop a concept that meets the requirements of the specification. Sometimes it may be necessary to change to a different concept if new information about the market, feasibility or cost is obtained.

- There is usually an embodiment stage of systems architecture, or layout design, of the new product's major subsystems and components before getting into detailed design. The 'look and feel' of the product is an important issue at this stage.

- It is necessary to build models and prototypes of the product to test for technical performance and to get feedback from potential purchasers and users. Computer modelling and rapid prototyping can make this much quicker and easier (as is outlined in Section 3 below).

- It is essential to design the selected concept in detail to satisfy materials and manufacturing requirements, as well as market and user requirements. This requires designers to have knowledge of materials and manufacturing processes. Costing of the product is vital to assess whether it is possible to satisfy these requirements.

- Designers need to consider the requirements of standards, regulations and legislation throughout the NPD process.

> Some of these lessons, especially those concerning the specification, concept and embodiment phases of the NPD process, should be useful in planning and carrying out your own project work.

Figure 13

2.2.3 Business activity models

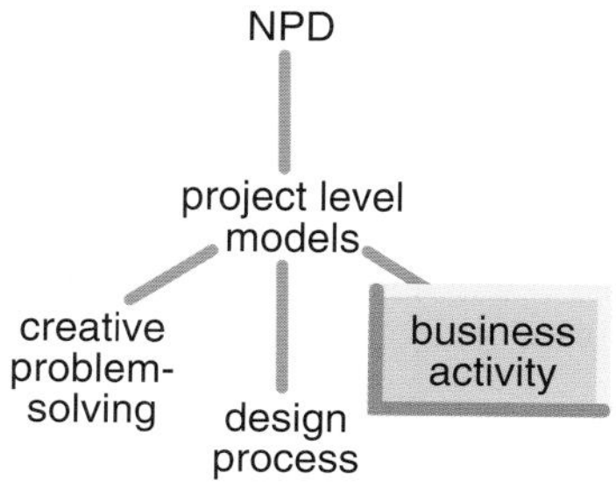

Design and development is at the core of the NPD process. For an independent inventor or designer this is often their main concern. However, as the *Invention and innovation* and *Markets* blocks showed, if they wish to succeed commercially with their proposed new product, an inventor or designer neglects business aspects at their peril. In commercial organisations, however, NPD normally involves business and market analysis and production planning before manufacture and market launch can take place. Business-activity models (Figure 13)

of product development tend to place as much, or more, emphasis on those management and planning activities as on the technical processes of product design and development.

One of the most widely used business activity models of NPD is the stage-gate model developed by Robert G. Cooper and described in his book *Winning at New Products* (Cooper, 2001). Its aim is to provide manufacturers with a systematic procedure to develop new products smoothly and rapidly from initial idea to market launch, and to reduce the risk of market failure.

The stage-gate system breaks an NPD project into discrete stages with management gates (decision points) before each one. In Cooper's (2001, p. 130) model there are five stages and gates, preceded by 'discovery' and followed by 'post-launch review' stages (see Figure 14 and Box 2). Each stage is designed to provide the information needed to progress to the next gate. Each gate is a go/no-go decision point at which the project team provides senior managers with the necessary information to decide, using a set of criteria, whether or not to go to the next stage, refer back or stop the project. These regular quality checks ensure an NPD project only proceeds if it's likely to be worthwhile to make further investments of people, time and funds.

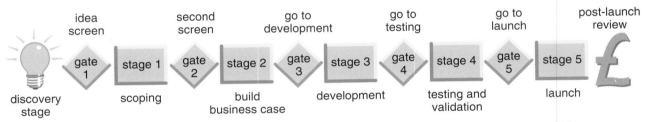

Figure 14 Generic stage-gate new product development process Source: adapted from Cooper, 2001

These investments grow rapidly as the project proceeds. For example, Hollins and Hollins (1991, p. 29) estimated that typically only about a quarter of the total cost of an NPD project occurs at the 'front end' market to concept design stages. Nearly two-thirds of the costs are spent in detail design and process engineering, and around 10 per cent in selling the finished product. Hollins and Hollins argue, in line with the stage-gate model, that more should be spent at the 'front end' to reduce the risk of commercial failure.

Box 2 Stage-gate model

Discovery stage

Pre-development work to discover and uncover new product opportunities and to generate ideas.

Gate 1 – idea screen

A preliminary 'gentle' screen signalling tentative commitment to the project if it meets criteria such as fit with company strategy, project feasibility and market attractiveness.

Stage 1 – scoping

A quick preliminary investigation of the technical merits of the project and its market prospects. Largely desk research.

Gate 2 – second screen

A more rigorous version of Gate 1.

Stage 2 – building the business case

A much more detailed investigation involving financial, market and technical feasibility studies, the development of market and technical specifications and a project plan. This is the critical homework stage – the one that makes or breaks the project.

Gate 3 – go to development

A yet more thorough screen of technical feasibility and market prospects together with financial evaluations and establishment of the product development team.

Stage 3 – development

The actual detailed design and development of the new product and the design of the manufacturing process.

Gate 4 – go to testing

A post-development review of the product and the project and whether they meet the required specifications and financial criteria. Approval of testing and validation plans.

Stage 4 – testing and validation

Tests or trials in the marketplace; laboratory and trial production plant to verify and validate the new product and its marketing and manufacturing.

Gate 5 – go to launch

An assessment of the results of testing and validation. The final opportunity to stop the project before full commercialisation.

Stage 5 – launch

Commercialisation of the product – the beginning of full manufacturing, marketing and selling.

Post-launch review

A review of the performance of the product and project – and a plan for improvement of the product.

(adapted from Cooper, 2001, pp. 131–41)

In the stage-gate model the 'discovery' stage is a crucial activity that starts the whole process. This is the stage at which ideas, market opportunities and inventions that may lead to a commercial new product are identified. As you've seen, ideas for new products may come from many sources, some mainly 'technology-push', others mainly 'market-pull' oriented. But notice that the actual design and development core of NPD (outlined earlier in Box 1) doesn't occur until stage 3 – after considerable business, market and technical evaluation has been carried out. The aim is to reduce the chance of commercial failure before making major investments in product development.

There is another crucial preparatory stage not formally included in the stage-gate model, namely formulating a *product* or *innovation strategy* – like the planning stage in the MIT design process model (see Figure 9b). Formulating a product or innovation strategy is a higher-level business activity than the stage-gate process and forms the context for specific NPD projects. This stage will be discussed in Section 4 below.

Cooper's stage-gate process, or variations of it, has been adopted by many companies. As you can see, it has much in common with the design process models, but with more emphasis on business, financial and commercial considerations. However, like the design process models, the stage-gate model is an idealised one and does not always neatly match what happens in real projects. In fact, Cooper suggests the number of stages and gates need not be rigid. Different organisations can and should adapt the model to their own needs, for example combining stage 1 (scoping) and stage 2 (business case) and combining stage 3 (product development) and stage 4 (testing), especially where less risky or ambitious projects are involved.

Even so, studies of actual projects have shown one or more of the key stage-gate activities (especially detailed market studies, test marketing and trial production) are frequently omitted or done inadequately, often with the result that the product fails, or is less commercially successful than it might have been.

So I'll look at another real-world case study, also of an innovative garden product (adapted from a book by Tim Jones, 1997).

After the case study there is an exercise for you to do, which you may wish to look at first.

Case study   Flymo Garden Vac

Background

Flymo is a UK-based manufacturer of garden products. Since 1964 the company has developed an innovative product range comprising electric and petrol driven hover mowers, wheeled rotary mowers, lawn trimmers, hedge-trimmers and, from spring 1993, the Garden Vac [Figures 15 and 16]. As part of the multinational Electrolux organization since 1968, their products are now sold in Europe, the United States, South Africa, Australia and the Far East. [...]

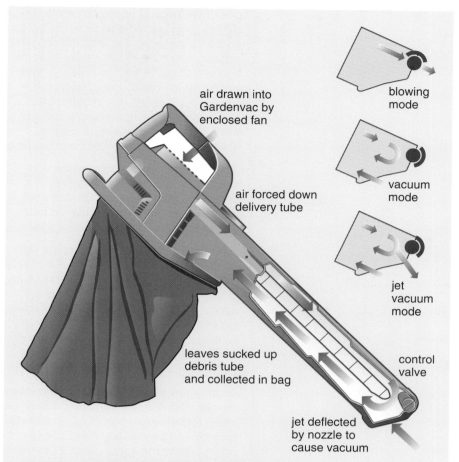

air drawn into
Gardenvac by
enclosed fan

blowing
mode

air forced down
delivery tube

vacuum
mode

jet
vacuum
mode

leaves sucked up
debris tube
and collected in bag

control
valve

jet deflected
by nozzle to
cause vacuum

Figure 15 Principle of the Flymo Garden Vac Source: Jones, 1997, p. 52, adapted from original from Flymo Ltd

In the late 1980s the Flymo-Electrolux group investigated the potential market available for [new] garden care products [to add to the range and extend their sales into the autumn], and, following detailed research, focused on the consumer demand for a garden 'tidy' product. Specifically they identified the need for an easy to use, competitively priced, all-purpose tool that could clear leaves, collect litter and tidy up trimmings from hedges and lawn borders.

During the 1980s there had been a significant growth in the sales of conventional blowers in the United States. [...] By 1990 it was apparent to Electrolux and, as part of the same group, Flymo, that the UK garden tidy market was therefore one of significant untapped potential. [...] However, to enter this market, they had to choose between either importing and branding an existing US product or manufacturing their own. If they were to take the second route, they could either design a new product themselves or, alternatively, acquire an innovative product from outside the company and then develop it internally. They chose the latter option.

This case history describes the invention and design of an innovative garden tidy product by a sole individual, its acquisition by an established manufacturer, its subsequent development and successful launch onto the market.

The idea

In autumn 1989 John Coathupe was a senior training officer in the north west of England, supervising engineering apprenticeships ... he owned one of the original Flymo hover mowers that, although proficient at cutting grass, would also blow the cut grass not just onto his lawn but also onto the drive and onto the soil where it was difficult to pick up. In addition, as many of the leaves from the trees in his garden were small, they were very difficult to brush up and, in the wet, were frequently walked inside the house ... he therefore looked for a product that would pick up such debris, but could not find one: although traditional blower products were being manufactured and sold in the US, at that time they were not readily available in Europe. Therefore ... he started to think how leaves and grass cuttings could be collected most efficiently.

[The case study then details how John Coathupe had the idea and through experimentation with many 'principle proving' models and prototypes invented a device that used the movement of air blown down a tube by an old vacuum cleaner, that was then redirected to create a partial vacuum and hence could suck up grass and leaves (Figure 15).]

John next built a full-size prototype, and, to make it easy to model ... used primarily balsa wood. As the possibility of using the invention to pick up litter as well as grass cuttings and leaves was then realized, this prototype was designed to pick up a drinks can. [...] Although to create the airflow, the end product would have an integral motor located at the top of the main tube near to the handle, for simplicity, this prototype continued to use the ... external power supply of the vacuum cleaner.

Patenting and licensing

As the product was plainly highly innovative and could have significant market potential, it was quickly determined that it was necessary to protect it by filing a patent application. [...] in February 1990 the prototype, drawings and descriptions of how it worked were taken to [a] patent agent, the specification drawn up and the patent application filed. This gave [John] a maximum of twelve months before the more costly applications for similar protection outside the UK would have to be made.

[...] By now well aware of how innovative a product he had invented, John had to decide whether he was going to develop it further himself ... or whether to try to license it to an existing manufacturer. Given the significant resources required to manufacture, promote and distribute such a product, he chose the second option. [...].

Over the next few weeks additional information was sent and the prototype was demonstrated to both Electrolux and Black & Decker. Initially Electrolux saw this as a product that would be most appropriate in their Floor-care division ... as a vacuum cleaner for use outside ... Taking along bags of polystyrene strips, dried leaves, grass cuttings, pieces of paper and crushed cans ... John initially showed it to Geoff Brewin, product engineering manager and a few weeks later to the [Floor-care] division's product review committee ... the prototype was also taken to Black & Decker's outdoor products division ... and shown to the head of R&D.

Both companies were impressed by the performance of the prototype and were sufficiently interested in the product's potential to offer to develop it further and make some fully working prototypes. [...] In the end the decision was made to go with Electrolux because ... only the Electrolux group would also have the capacity to manufacture [both electric and] petrol driven versions, thereby, in John's opinion, offering a ... greater potential market for the product.

It was agreed that Electrolux Floor-care would undertake some market testing and examine how well the product could fit into the company's product range. In addition they would also make a number of development models to assess whether it was both technically feasible and manufacturable and also determine potential performance characteristics. This was done with the assistance of an external design group, who produced two working prototypes from thermoplastic sheeting. [...]

Unfortunately, in December 1990, after six months development and evaluation, Electrolux Floor-care decided not to go ahead with the project. Although they had confirmed that the product was technically viable and could potentially be manufactured at a realistic cost, after carrying out initial hall tests [in which prototypes were shown to potential customers – see the *Markets* block], they had reservations about its market potential. Fundamentally it was not felt to fit in with the rest of their portfolio of vacuuming products. Geoff Brewin however was convinced of the product's potential and [...] redirected the project to Flymo for evaluation as a garden only product [...]

[Here the case study describes further approaches and offers to develop the product by Black & Decker and the British Technology Group.]

While John was weighing up these two options, [the] product planning manager at Flymo asked for a demonstration ... Flymo had independently completed a survey of the potential for a garden tidy product in the European market and had been looking at a number of options. They were in the process of evaluating whether to brand one of the existing Electrolux owned Poulan-Weedeater products, develop an improved version of a US product to overcome an identified problem of clogging by wet leaves, or alternatively, develop their own new product for which a number of concepts had been generated internally. So, when the information about the Garden Vac – a 'clean fan' solution potentially better than existing 'dirty fan' US products [which suck leaves etc. through the fan] was passed across from the Floor-care division, Flymo were very keen to see it...

So in February 1991, John faced another choice, now between three offers: from Black & Decker, the British Technology Group and Flymo. He chose the latter. [...] Flymo were clearly very keen to back the product by providing all the necessary resources, funding its development and initiating an extensive high profile marketing campaign [...] The invention was therefore licensed to Flymo and both the original balsa model and the prototypes made for Electrolux Floor-care were handed over for further development in February 1991.

Development

[...] The design was first assessed in detail from an ergonomic perspective with different configurations of the tube, handle and motor being evaluated to determine the optimum solution in terms of balance and ease of use....

In addition, experiments were undertaken with different sizes and shapes of the nozzle [...] [A rotating valve to provide a blow function was added.]

Next an additional feature, the jet vacuum, was also introduced to overcome an identified problem with wet leaves... by bleeding off a little air from the main flow in vacuum mode, a powerful jet of air flowing through a small slot in the control valve could be created. This would help to chisel or turn up the edges of any leaves... to successfully pick up the leaves off the ground. Again after modelling and testing, this additional feature was also incorporated within the evolving product ...

The other key development work undertaken at this stage was the determination of precise power requirements and the sourcing of an appropriate motor. [...]

In October 1991, the results of these assessments and the original prototypes were handed over to an internal development team whose responsibility it was to turn the working prototypes into a manufacturable product which met all the appropriate standards, could be easily assembled and would achieve the planned ex-works target cost thus enabling it to be sold for a desired £79. [...]

Flymo then involved an external industrial design consultancy, Renfrew Associates, to provide an input to the styling of the product. ... the industrial designers at Renfrew were able to work on the overall external shape to produce a design which would both enhance market perceptions of an innovative product and fit into the developing Flymo product range ... and by the end of January 1992 had produced a full scale mock-up of the proposed design.

[Here the case study briefly outlines the development of tooling to mould the production samples in ABS plastic.]

The first samples were used by the development team to build initial products to evaluate product performance and check that all the mouldings fitted within planned tolerances. Further mouldings were then used for a pre-production build by manufacturing to test their assembly line in February, leading to the commencement of full scale production in March 1993 ... .

Figure 16 Flymo Garden Vac: improved Garden Vac 1800 Plus with integral shredder Source: Flymo Ltd

Product performance

At the time of its launch in March 1993, the UK market for conventional blowervacs imported from the US was only 5000 units a year. Within six months Flymo were selling this many a week and by the end of the first year had sold 200 000. They had invested in a high profile TV advertising campaign which ... helped sales ...

In reaction to this success, Black & Decker quickly imported and re-engineered one of their existing traditional US products to compete in the UK market but were unable to catch up with Flymo who, having successfully persuaded Weedeater to factor the Garden Vac as a premium product in the USA and Canada, by mid-1995 had sold over 1 million units worldwide. [...]

Continued innovation

Like other successful manufacturers, Flymo on average launch six new products every year to maintain their lead in the market. Since the launch of the first Garden Vac product in March 1993, they have been working on a range of further innovations and the first of these was introduced in summer 1995. The only advantage that the traditional US blowervac products had over the original Garden Vac was that, through utilising the 'dirty fan' principle, they automatically mulched any debris collected. [...] to provide this additional facility ... eight months after launch, Flymo began working on the inclusion of one of their other areas of core technology into a second generation of the product (Figure 16) ... By incorporating a mono-filament cutting line used in their trimmers at the top of the main tube and driving it from the same motor as the fan, they created a product which not only shredded grass cuttings, leaves and litter, but one which could also allow solid debris such as twigs and cans to pass straight through into the collecting bag. This incremental improvement helped Flymo to maintain their dominance of this sector of the market and was the first of a number of innovations to be introduced over the following years.

(adapted from Jones, 1997, pp. 52–63)

Exercise 3   Garden Vac – theory and practice

Look back over the stage-gate model of NPD and the Garden Vac case study. Identify some of the similarities and differences between the idealised stage-gate model and the case study of the invention, development and launch of the Flymo Garden Vac. Also, try to identify how well the development of the Garden Vac fits any one of the design process models of NPD discussed earlier.

Spend about 20–25 minutes on this exercise before looking at the discussion below.

Discussion

As with most actual cases of new product development or innovation, the story of the development of the Flymo Garden Vac is more complex than can be explained by the idealised stage-gate or design process models of NPD. Nevertheless, several features of these models are noticeable.

Product and innovation strategy

Prior to the project, Electrolux-Flymo had already identified a need for new garden products as a result of carrying out market studies ('Specifically they identified the need for an easy to use, competitively priced, all-purpose tool that could clear leaves, collect litter and tidy up trimmings from hedges and lawn borders...'.)

Discovery – idea screen (pre-development stage – gate 1)

The project started outside the group with an invention by an independent engineer. He identified a potential market for a garden tidy product from personal experience, created the inventive principle and had already done some of the initial concept and embodiment design work to produce a rough balsa wood prototype. His own technical and market analysis led him to offer his invention to the Electrolux group for development and manufacture. The invention seemed to fit Electrolux's product strategy, by offering the potential to extend their range. So there was a promising idea to start a stage-gate type NPD process within a business.

A demonstration of the prototype to the product review committee of Electrolux's Floor-care division allowed the idea/invention to pass 'gate 1'. (They 'were impressed by the performance of the prototype and were sufficiently interested in the product's potential to offer to develop it further and make some fully working prototypes'.)

Scoping – second screen (stage 1 – gate 2)

Electrolux Floor-care then conducted a stage 1 scoping study: a quick and inexpensive assessment of the technical merits of the project and its market prospects. ('They would also make a number of development models to assess whether it was both technically feasible and manufacturable.')

However, the prototype designs failed to pass Electrolux Floor-care's 'gate 2' for reasons of market potential and product strategy.

Build business case – go to development (stage 2 – gate 3)

The project then was passed on to Flymo that had already conducted its own pre-development discovery and stage 1 scoping work and was ready to begin moving towards a stage 2 detailed investigation of the novel 'clean fan' Garden Vac prototype.

According to the case study, Flymo's stage 2 investigation seemed to focus mainly on technical feasibility and further embodiment design work and to do little in the way of detailed financial and market assessments.

The product seems to have passed successfully through gate 3 – decision on the business case – although this is not described in the case study and may have been less formal and rigorous than recommended in the stage-gate model, because it is at this point that significant amounts of resources are committed.

Development – go to testing (stage 3 – gate 4)

The project then moved to stage 3 development where the emphasis is on technical and design development, consumer feedback and planning for manufacture and sale: '...the original prototypes were handed over to an internal development team whose responsibility it was to turn the working prototypes into a manufacturable product ... Flymo then involved an external industrial design consultancy, Renfrew Associates, to provide an input to the styling of the product.'

While the technical aspects of stage 3 were clearly undertaken, by a multidisciplinary project team, it isn't clear from the case study whether any customer feedback on the developing product design was obtained.

Testing and validation – go to launch (stage 4 – gate 5)

According to the case study, from this point the project seems to have moved rapidly through the areas covered by stage 4-gate 5: testing and validation of the project and the product, the production process, customer acceptance, and the economics of the project.

The case study briefly outlines the development of tooling to mould pre-production samples in ABS plastic.

It seems Flymo was confident enough in the success of its new product that it proceeded to finalise the design, order the tooling, do a pre-production trial and commence manufacture without necessarily carrying out all the detailed financial and market, as well as technical, tests and checks recommended in the stage-gate model. However Flymo had already calculated a target manufacturing cost and sales price of £79 that must have involved financial and market analysis. Flymo's confidence seems to have been justified in that the Garden Vac quickly became one of its most successful products.

Launch – post-launch review (stage 5 – post-development stage)

After stage 5, as recommended in the stage-gate model, Flymo kept the new product's performance in the market under review. As a result, the company introduced a series of incremental improvements to the design, starting with the Garden Vac Plus that could both collect and shred grass, leaves and other garden litter.

Conclusion

The Garden Vac case study does exhibit many of the elements of both the stage-gate and design process models of new product development. However, the project is more complex than these models suggest because the new product was initially developed by an inventor and then developed further by two companies within the Electrolux/Flymo group.

The technical and business activities undertaken by Flymo broadly, although not exactly, follow those recommended in the models. But it appears, at least from the case study, there was a greater focus on technical design and development, especially after the initial stages, and less business analysis and market testing and fewer formal go/no-go 'gates' than recommended by the stage-gate model. Perhaps Flymo was lucky with this project, or maybe its business and market evaluations at the early stages allowed the company to proceed confidently to manufacture and market launch.

What further lessons about successful NPD can you draw from the stage-gate model and the Garden Vac case?

- An independent inventor or designer can normally only go so far in developing a new technical product, often to the 'principle-proving' model or working prototype stage. Beyond that, the resources and skills required usually require the involvement of one or more companies and/or design consultancy firms.

- Valuable ideas for new products can come from sources external to a company. Successful businesses are open to ideas and products to develop or adapt from any promising internal or external source.

- Before a company starts an NPD project, it should first satisfy itself that the planned product supports its product strategy.

- The likely market demand and financial costs and returns of designing, manufacturing and selling a new product should be assessed before investing in its development.

- Increasing the relatively small investments at the 'front end' of NPD can help to reduce the risks of commercial failure. Testing customer responses to prototypes before going to production also helps reduce the risk of failure.

- As well as financial assessments, NPD projects should include regular technical and commercial progress checks by senior decision makers and the project modified, or even abandoned, if necessary.

Some of these lessons, especially those concerning the specification to embodiment phases of the NPD process, should be useful in planning and carrying out your own project work.

2.3 Designing service products

So far I've discussed the design and development of manufactured products. But an increasing proportion of NPD involves the design of service products, such as banking and insurance products, hotel and catering services, leisure and tourism packages, retail outlets, and cleaning and maintenance systems. In addition, even manufacturers increasingly offer their customers total 'solutions', for example a car with financing, maintenance and insurance included in the price. There isn't room in this block to discuss the design of service products, which are usually a mix of intangible service elements, physical products and equipment and, often, computer software.

A good example of an innovative service product is the 'Umbrolly' vending machine business, conceived by Charles Ejogo (after he had been caught in the rain) to sell low-cost umbrellas and other products at stations and elsewhere. The new service involved the development of novel plasma screen vending machines (Figure 17) as well as establishing the business.

Hollins and Hollins (1991, p. 18) have shown that the early phases of the design process models (market research, specification, concept design) are valid for the creation and development of service products, with an implementation phase replacing the manufacture and sell phases. They give an example of this process applied to the design of a carpet-cleaning service. Also, the creative problem solving model can be used to the generate ideas for new service products, while a stage-gate approach is useful for checking that commercial issues are fully considered during the development process.

In Part 2, using ideas about the design of service products, I shall introduce some concepts for new systems of products and services ('sustainable innovations') that could radically reduce environmental impacts; for example leasing centres for supplying and caring for clothes. These are also examples of configurational innovations, because they involve changes in both technology and organisation.

Figure 17 Vending machine with plasma advertising screen developed for the Umbrolly low-cost umbrella sales service at London Underground stations and elsewhere Source: Umbrolly

Key points of Section 2

- There are many models of the NPD process, each describing aspects of the process but with a different focus. No single model fully describes the NPD process; successful real-world projects usually include elements of the different types – creative problem solving; a systematic design process, and stage-gate management.

- The models can provide valuable lessons and guidelines to help in managing and carrying out practical NPD projects, including your own project work.

- It is vital to get the initial stages of the NPD process correct. No product, however well designed in detail, will succeed if the basic idea or concept design is flawed from a technical or market viewpoint. Investment in the 'front end' of NPD is worthwhile to increase the likelihood of product success.

- Key elements of a successful NPD project include:

  – a clear technical and market specification

  – a concept design and a working embodiment or prototype that meet the specification

  – a detailed design that satisfies potential purchasers and users, meets required safety and environmental standards, conforms to regulations and legislation, and ensures economic manufacture.

- Continuous improvement of an innovative product is usually needed to ensure its long-term success, especially if rival products already exist or are launched by competitors.

- Many NPD projects involve service products, whose development can be based on models similar to those used for designing manufactured products.

3 Organisation for new product development

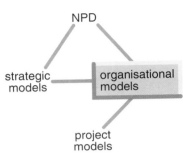

Figure 18

One reason for the success of the Garden Vac was Flymo's use of a multidisciplinary team to design and develop the product. So I'll turn now to the organisational models (Figure 18) that are concerned with different ways people can be organised and managed to carry out new product development projects.

3.1 Concurrent product development

The models you have encountered so far may appear to be linear or sequential, showing new product development as a series of activities following one after the other. For example, in a traditional linear model of NPD, the marketing department provides a brief or market specification to a company's designers and engineers, who then create and develop a design that is then passed to the production engineers to convert into a product that can be manufactured. This approach has been likened to a 'relay race' in which each department in an organisation makes its contribution in isolation before passing the baton (representing the project) to the next department (Figure 19a).

In reality, as you should have realised from my examples and case studies (and perhaps from your own project work), NPD is usually more complex than this with much backtracking and feedback between activities. This has given rise to iterative models of product development that, continuing the sporting analogy, have been likened to a 'volleyball game'. Here, product development proceeds through a series of iterative loops, during which the product may be passed back and forth between departments and modified several times, before being ready for the next stage of development (Figure 19b).

Volleyball NPD and even relay race NPD still occur in some organisations. However, these approaches are now generally recognised as being outdated and inefficient, causing unnecessary delays and insufficient interaction between marketing, design and manufacturing functions needed to produce well-designed, high-quality, economic products matched to customer needs. Rapid product development has become essential to ensure products reach the market on time, perhaps before competitors do so with rival products. It is also vital for financial reasons, because the sales returns on the investment in product development and manufacturing do not start until the product diffuses into the market. Finally, it is important because by reducing product development times an organisation should be able to develop, introduce and market more new products within a given period.

To speed product development integrated approaches to NPD have emerged. In these approaches the different phases of product development overlap or take place in parallel. This is made possible by the individuals and departments involved working together as a team. In my sporting analogy, this approach has been compared to a 'rugby team' in which the members of a multidisciplinary, or cross-functional, product development team work together passing the ball (representing the project) back and forth as they move forward (Figure 19c).

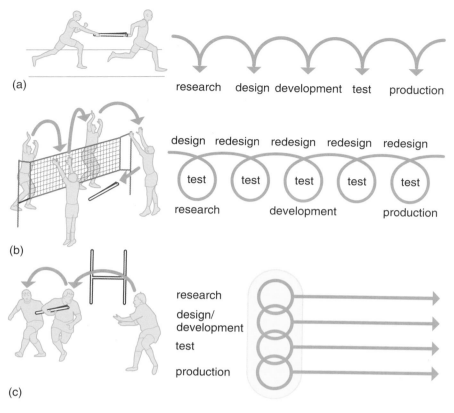

research   design   development   test   production

design   redesign   redesign   redesign   redesign

test   test   test   test   test

research   development   production

research

design/
development

test

production

Figure 19 **Sporting analogies for the NPD process: (a) the relay race is where the traditional linear or sequential approach means each department makes its contribution in isolation before passing the project to the next department; (b) the volleyball game is where product development proceeds through iterative loops before moving to the next department; (c) the rugby game is where a cross-functional team work together on product development, passing the project back and forth as they proceed**
Sources: (a–c) adapted from Open University, 1996, p. 55, after Winstanley and Francis, 1988

3.2   Product development teams

The team-based, integrated approach was pioneered by Japanese car manufacturers, led by Toyota, in the 1980s. It was part of Toyota's lean production system that integrated manufacturing expertise, such as the development of dies used to press car body parts, with the design of the car bodies themselves. Since then, the change to so-called concurrent engineering has been made by most major European and US companies, as well as by many smaller ones. Concurrent engineering is also referred to as simultaneous engineering.

Although the stage-gate product development process introduced in Section 2 and used by many companies, appears linear with one stage following another, in practice it is a concurrent process normally undertaken by a team with members from all the relevant functional areas. Likewise, the gates are staffed by senior decision makers from the different functional departments who control the resources needed to proceed to the next stage. Shetty (2002, p. 19) notes that:

> Use of cross-functional product development teams has a major effect on both time and quality. With people from different functions working together, development gets done faster because

concurrent engineering

team-based approach to the simultaneous, integrated design of products and their related processes, to accelerate development and improve quality activities can be done in parallel rather than in series. Quality improves because people from different functions work together to understand and solve development problems...Team members come from functions such as marketing, design, service, quality, manufacturing, engineering, testing and purchasing... sometimes customer representatives also are included, allowing the voice of the customer to be heard throughout the development process. Team members work together, sharing information and knowledge, and producing better results faster than they would have done if operating in traditional product development.

While concurrent or simultaneous engineering is an ideal, in practice it's not usually possible to carry out all the product development tasks in parallel and so 'phase overlapping' is a more accurate description of what usually happens.

product creation process

another term for new product development, usually involving a concurrent engineering approach

At Royal Philips Electronics for example, the product creation process (PCP) comprises a series of phases that overlap (interpenetrate) to a greater or lesser extent and to which every relevant discipline contributes throughout (Figure 20). This led Muller (2004) to write that PCP within Philips is 'a synchronized effort of nearly all disciplines'. Although there are no formal 'gates', progress is checked at the transition from one phase to the next and management approval is required for significant investments.

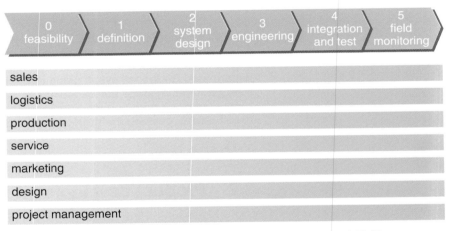

Figure 20   Phases of the product creation process at Royal Philips Electronics, showing the overlapping of phases and participation of all relevant disciplines during the entire process Source: Muller, 2004, p. 2

Case study   JCB Teletruk

The Teletruk, launched in 1997, was part of JCB's strategy to expand from earth-moving and agricultural machinery into forklift trucks. However, the forklift sector is mature and highly competitive, so JCB knew it had to create an innovative design in order to break profitably into this market. The company did this by first conducting an initial business and market appraisal. Although this indicated the major investment required to develop a new forklift would not be recovered for several years, JCB's chairman decided to go ahead, relying on the company's ability to innovate and to control costs by using existing components in a new design.

A dedicated 12-person team was set up to carry out the project. The team included people new to this type of work, who took a radical approach to forklift truck design involving use of a single telescopic arm from existing JCB machines (Figure 21). Many other components, such as the engine and transmission, were also from other JCB vehicles.

Figure 21   The JCB Teletruk has a novel side-mounted telescopic boom in place of the conventional forklift truck mast, which improves driver visibility and enables the truck to operate in confined spaces
Source: JCB

(Based on Jolly, 2003, pp. 8–9; 83–4)

There was a formal project plan controlled using standard computer-scheduling software and the team reported its progress at key stages to senior management. Suppliers and partners, and an external design consultancy firm, provided expert inputs to the project, and signed confidentiality agreements, so that competitors did not learn about the Teletruk's novel design. Throughout the project the team adopted a user-centred design approach, which you can read about in more detail in the Design Council Teletruk case study on the T211 DVD.

Despite its higher price than conventional forklift trucks, the Teletruk has sold well and the design has been tailored to suit individual customer's requirements

3.2.1 Suppliers and specialists

So far, I've discussed the product development team as if most of its members come from one organisation. However, it has become beyond the capabilities of most companies to develop new products or innovations on their own, and the 'extended team' normally includes the company's suppliers (Figure 22). NPD has therefore become the task of a network or 'supply chain', comprising a manufacturer such as JCB, Flymo or Philips, its 'first tier' suppliers of subsystems, components and materials, and second and third tier suppliers to the first tier suppliers. Moreover, NPD is often not so much the responsibility of individual manufacturers as of partnerships or 'strategic alliances' of companies – often former competitors such as Philips and Sony – and their network of suppliers.

Universities, government laboratories, research institutes, technical consultants and research, design and development firms, such as IDEO, have often replaced the work of in-house R&D laboratories, which many large companies have scaled down or even closed (Broers, 2005). Industrial design consultants may be involved to provide

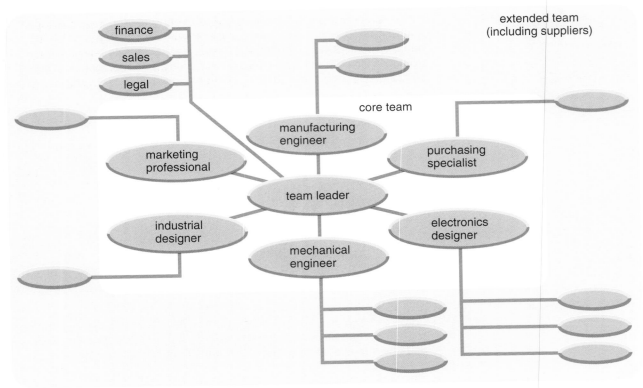

Figure 22 Composition of a product development team for an electromechanical product of modest complexity Source: adapted from Ulrich and Eppinger, 2000, p. 5

specialist design inputs on the 'look and feel' and ergonomics of a product, as in the cases of the Teletruck and Garden Vac.

It's not only large companies that develop their products in collaboration with others. Individual inventors and designers and small companies also usually need to obtain help and collaboration from suppliers, universities and/or consultants when developing a new product; as in the case of the Garden Groom. Small companies, inventors and designers also provide inputs as suppliers and consultants to large manufacturers' NPD projects.

Rothwell (1992) was one of the first to identify this emerging collaborative approach to product development, which he named the systems integration and networking (SIN) model.

systems integration and networking model

builds on concurrent engineering to include strategic partnerships with suppliers and customers together with collaborative research and marketing

3.2.2 Team communications

An important issue is how best to facilitate good communication between members of a product development team, including suppliers. One way is to place the team members physically together in the same building (so-called collocation). In some companies collocation has involved major investments— for example, in 1990 the German car manufacturer BMW opened its new Research and Innovation centre, designed to facilitate close collaboration between all the various groups involved in product development and innovation:

Here, some 7,000 engineers, prototype builders, computer experts, and scientists from many areas – as well as purchasers and employees belonging to supplier companies ... develop vehicles and technologies of the future for the BMW group.

(a)

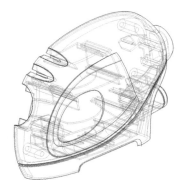

(b)

(c)

Figure 23   Using computers in product design and development to increase quality and to reduce concept-to-market lead times: (a) 3D solid model of a Black & Decker Mouse sander produced on a CAD system; (b) 3D hybrid surface computer model of Black & Decker Mouse sander; (c) resin appearance model of a glue gun produced by stereolithography addition (SLA); this type of rapid prototyping enables a CAD model to be quickly made into a physical model Source: Open University, 2004c, p. 87, 99

computer-aided design

computer software tools used to generate ideas, 2D and 3D models, and to incorporate component and material data

The honeycomb-shaped building complex is arranged in open modules, giving employees close proximity to others. [...] This means that all three functional areas – development, manufacture, and purchasing – work very closely with each other... Even suppliers are incorporated within the teams through Simultaneous Engineering.

(http://www.bmwgroup.com/e/nav/index.html [accessed 19.7.05])

As well as collocating researchers, designers and engineers, innovative businesses, like Dyson Ltd, and design consultancy firms, like IDEO, also place much emphasis on providing office environments in which product development team members can work and relax together in an informal and creative atmosphere.

Increasingly, however, given the networking approach to NPD, teams are becoming 'virtual'. Teams may have members located at different sites of the same company, involve scientists, designers, engineers and marketers from several companies who are collaborating on a project, and include suppliers located in many different countries, such as China and India. These virtual teams communicate via a variety of electronic media such as email, computer conferencing, Powerpoint presentations, shared databases and intranets linking designers, manufacturers and their network of suppliers.

IDEO describes its NPD process as rather like making a film, 'you pick the best, assemble a team, work intensively for a few months and then disband. Depending on the project there may be a scramble of people moving from one office to another. Other times people in different cities work together, via email, conferencing, or our Intranet.'

(Myerson, 2001)

Even BMW with its central Research and Innovation centre is increasingly relying on electronic communications and shared computing:

... new [product] development processes involve seeing to it that as many individual tasks as possible are accomplished simultaneously ... All participants in this process, including suppliers, are in constant contact with one another. Innovative technical and computer-supported methods support this process. Today, not one series vehicle developed by the BMW group hasn't been imaged, tested and optimised virtually – before becoming a reality.

(http://www.bmwgroup.com/e/nav/index.html, [accessed 19.7.05])

3.2.3 Computer tools

As you've seen, companies are increasingly dependent on networked computers for communications. Computers of course are involved in many other NPD tasks. These include project planning and control, storing and accessing information via databases, the generation of designs, testing by computer simulation and producing physical models and prototypes.

In computer-aided design (CAD) 2D and 3D virtual models of a concept, product or component are generated and manipulated on screen, allowing a large number of alternative designs to be explored

simulation

developing, testing and studying a computer model of a product, component or process before it is created

rapid prototyping

process that builds a physical prototype in resin or other material directly from the digital information in a computer model

rapidly (see Figure 10c and Figure 23a). Simulation is used to study the performance of a product, component or process before it has been physically made or implemented by developing and testing it using a computer model (Figure 23b). In rapid prototyping a physical prototype of a product or component is produced in resin or other material directly from a computer model (Figure 23c). Another major benefit of designing by computer is that the resultant computer model can be linked from a computer aided design and manufacturing (CADCAM) system directly to production equipment, even that located in factories of distant suppliers.

The IDEO video on the T211 DVD and the videos 'Philips: creative product design' and 'Philips: new product development' on the T211 and T307 DVDs show the use of multidisciplinary teams to undertake NPD projects.

The T211 DVD also includes professional-standard computer tools for designers and engineers – CES Selector and solidThinking. Even if you don't have time to learn to use it, you can set solidThinking to demonstrate what such 3D CAD software can do.

Use all this material at a convenient point during your study of this section and/or while working on your project.

3.3 NPD organisation

As you've seen, concurrent approaches to NPD use a multidisciplinary or cross-functional project team to undertake most of the tasks involved. But dedicated project teams are not the only way in which new product development may be organised. An independent inventor or designer, or individuals in a small enterprise, do not require a formal organisation for product development. However, if the enterprise grows into a medium or large company, some form of organisational, or management, structure is necessary.

In any NPD project a variety of functional specialists may be required. These will usually include marketers, designers, and manufacturing engineers; and often purchasing, finance and sales staff; and sometimes strategic planners, legal advisers, human factors experts, social scientists and environmental technologists (see Figure 22). The question is how best to organise them?

functional organisation

new products are developed in stages by specialist departments with functional managers

project organisation

new products are developed by a dedicated team under a project manager

strong matrix

project team led by a strong project manager, while links are kept with functional managers

3.3.1 Organisational structures

Figure 24 shows the essential features of the four main organisational or management structures for NPD. In the traditional functional organisation (Figure 24a) a new product is developed in stages via the different specialist departments. In the pure project organisation (Figure 24b) product development is undertaken by a dedicated team under a project manager. There are two types of *matrix* organisation: in a strong matrix (Figure 24c) specialist staff are temporarily assigned to work on a project under a 'heavyweight' project manager, while retaining links to their departments for training and promotion.

weak matrix

organisational structure where project team members remain within their functional departments and a project manager coordinates the work

In a weak matrix organisation (Figure 24d) a 'lightweight' project manager coordinates the work of project team members who remain within their functional departments. The strong matrix is therefore closer to a project organisation than the weak matrix.

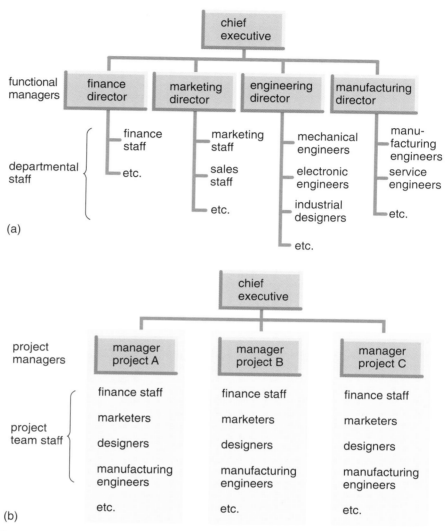

(a)

(b)

Figure 24   Four main types of organisational structure for NPD: (a) functional organisation; (b) project organisation; (c) strong matrix organisation; (d) weak matrix organisation Sources: (a–d) Open University, 2001b, pp. 123–5, based on Open University, 1996, pp. 26–7

Choosing an organisational structure

The choice of an appropriate organisational structure for an NPD project depends on a number of factors, including the history, size and culture of the company – or network of companies – involved, and the complexity of the project. There are no ideal solutions, but there are some guidelines that may be helpful.

Functional organisations

These foster deep specialist expertise in their departments, but coordination between different functions is often slow and bureaucratic. So an organisational structure based on functional

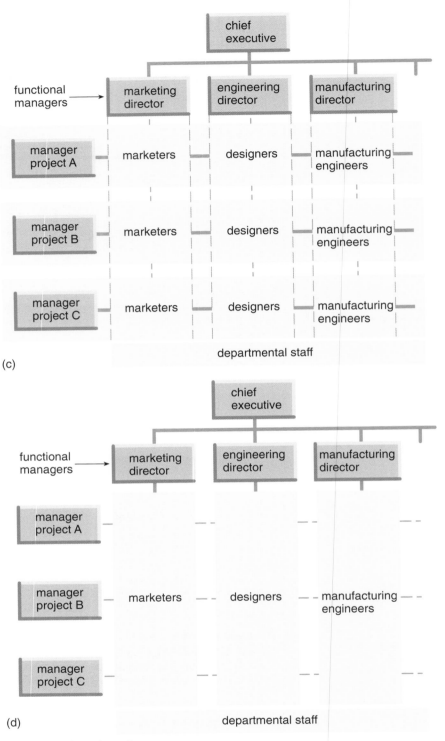

Figure 24 (continued)

departments and using a linear, relay race NPD process is only really suitable for routine projects involving little innovation. In such organisations attempts at innovative projects typically result in delays and cost overruns because key market, technical and design requirements are often missed, requiring redesign work to be carried out late in the development process.

Pure project organisations

These allow efficient coordination between the diverse functions required to carry out an NPD project. IDEO, for example, uses 'small, focused, autonomous teams of 2–6 people', supported by computer and communications technologies, which rapidly complete a project before its members move on to the next project. Project organisations are suited to innovative new products, as well as for large projects that justify employing specialists from different functional departments on a full-time basis. Even so, team members may not possess all the necessary specialist knowledge. A common hybrid type, therefore, is a project team that receives assistance from functional specialists (industrial designers, computer technicians, materials scientists, test engineers, and so on) who remain in their functional departments, are employed as consultants, or are provided by suppliers.

Matrix organisational structures (both strong and weak)

These methods of organisation were originally developed to deal with large aerospace projects. They can provide the advantages of both functional and project organisations, but at a cost of greater management effort and the potential for resource conflicts between functional and project managers and divided loyalties among team members. Matrix organisations are appropriate for large, complex projects requiring simultaneous inputs of specialists from several disciplines or departments, but who can't be spared full time for the duration of the project.

Table 1 outlines the strengths and weaknesses of the functional, project and matrix organisational structures for NPD.

Table 1   Organisational structures for NPD

	Functional organisation	Matrix organisation		Project organisation
		Weak	Strong	
Strengths	Fosters development of deep specialisation and expertise.	Coordination and administration of projects is explicitly assigned to a single project manager. Maintains development of specialization and expertise.	Provides integration and speed benefits of the project organisation. Some of the specialisation of a functional organisation is retained.	Resources can be optimally allocated within the project team. Technical and market trade-offs can be evaluated quickly.

	Functional organisation	Matrix organisation		Project organisation
		Weak	Strong	
Weaknesses	Coordination among different functional groups can be slow and bureaucratic.	Requires more managers and administrators than a non matrix organisation.		Individuals may have difficulty maintaining cutting-edge functional capabilities.
Typical examples	Companies in which development involves slight variations to a standard design (e.g. custom motors, bearings, packaging).	Traditional automobile, electronics, and aerospace companies.	Many recently successful projects in automobile, electronics, and aerospace companies.	Start-up companies. 'Tiger teams' and 'skunk works' intended to achieve breakthroughs. Companies in extremely dynamic markets.
Major issues	How to integrate different functions to achieve a common goal.	How to balance functions and projects. How to simultaneously evaluate project and functional performance.		How to maintain functional expertise over time. How to share technical learning from one project to another.

Source: adapted from Ulrich and Eppinger (2000) Exhibit 2–7, p. 29

Many variants and combinations of these four organisational structures are used in practice. Different structures may be employed at different stages of a project. A project organisation may be best when creating innovative product concepts, but the team may hand over to functional departments, or to another part of the business, to develop and manufacture the product.

The importance of choosing an appropriate organisational structure is illustrated dramatically by the abandonment of British Rail's Advanced Passenger Train (APT) project in the mid-1980s after 15 years of development work (Potter, 1986; Open University, 1999a). The APT, a highly innovative tilting train, started as an R&D project carried out by a dedicated team in BR's research department.

The problems began when the team was moved into BR's functionally organised engineering department to develop the experimental prototype into a working train. Many engineers were sceptical about the APT and so the team became isolated from the specialist train design and testing expertise in the Engineering department. The team was then split up in a reorganisation of the department into a kind of weak matrix organisation managed by a lightweight project manager, who could not gain the resources he needed to develop the APT to schedule.

When eventually the APT team was reorganised under a heavyweight project manager, and the production prototypes began running successfully, the economic case for high-speed tilting trains had weakened and the project was finally abandoned. Had the APT been developed via a strong matrix structure from the start, the outcome might have been different and APTs or their successors, rather than a design based on Italian Pendolino tilting trains, could be running on Britain's west coast main line.

The following case study shows a largely functional organisation can become more innovative by shifting to a more appropriate structure for NPD.

Case study | Creative project teams at Mattel

The US toy maker Mattel had a largely functional structure for product development and relied heavily on incremental design changes to its traditional brands such as the Barbie fashion doll range.

'The marketing department would pass on the business objectives to the design department. The designers there would create the visual [design] and then pass it to engineering who would in turn pass it to the packaging section. Each one competed with the other and worked in silos. Designers needed to let colleagues into their design process and try not to own it' (Zacharias, 2004, p. 3).

In 2001, following a sharp decline in demand for the Barbie range, the former head of design and development for the Girls Division of Mattel, Ivy Ross, set out to create a new toy for girls. Ross, frustrated by lack of creativity and innovation in the company, believed that a new approach to product development was required. Ross assembled an unofficial 12-person team with members drawn from several Mattel departments representing various backgrounds and skills. Working during lunch breaks, at nights and weekends, the team decided to create a different kind of toy for pre-teenage girls.

To help the group's thinking, Ross exposed them to a number of stimuli, such as an architect to talk about design and engineering principles and a performer to demonstrate free association of ideas. They observed a group of girls building with things like pipe cleaners and cardboard. Two weeks of 'mental grazing' prepared the group to begin creating their own ideas. Team members agreed to shed their titles and set their own schedules.

The result was the Ello Creation System launched in the US in 2002 and Europe in 2003. Ello has colourful panels, balls, miniature flowers and other pieces that can be used to build houses, people, pets, jewellery or anything else five- to ten-year-old girls might dream up (Figure 25).

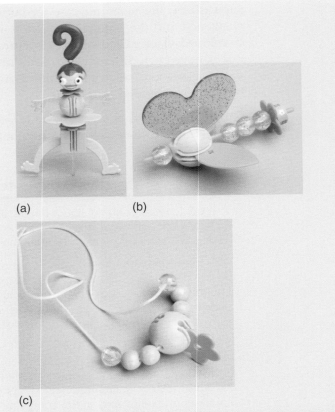

(a)   (b)

(c)

Figure 25   Mattel's Ello Creation System construction toy aimed at 5–10-year-old girls

Based upon the success of the Ello project, Mattel's chairman, Robert Eckert, endorsed Ross' proposal for official support of her dedicated team approach to design, which became known as 'Project Platypus'.

Unlike the Ello group, the Platypus teams were released from their regular jobs for twelve weeks and worked together in a studio near Mattel's California headquarters. Each session begins with what Ross calls 'grazing'. Outside speakers are brought in – during the first week to teach participants how to get into a creative thinking mode, and to give background market and technical information about the product category. The second week features speakers that relate to the project at hand. After the 'Platypi' have taken in the information, the creative work begins. The room has desks on wheels so people can literally link with whoever they feel like working with; and all ideas are posted on a wall. By the end of 2003, four groups had completed Project Platypus exercises; producing three more products that Mattel opted to develop. Meanwhile, Mattel added new ranges to its new Ello brand.

(Based on Lees, 2003; Thompson, 2004; and Zacharias, 2004)

Matching the complexity of project and organisation

As I mentioned earlier, a factor that influences the choice of organisational structure for NPD is the complexity of the project. Project complexity might be measured by the number of new subsystems and components that have to be integrated in the new product. It also depends on the complexity of the organisation(s) in which the project is carried out, measured for example by the number of participants involved.

To carry out a complex, innovative project, like the APT discussed above, is likely to require an organisational structure, such as a strong matrix, that matches the project's complexity. In the APT case this did not happen until too late, for a variety of factors to do with the culture and organisation within British Rail at the time.

As the following case study – of another high-speed train development – shows, in large international NPD projects the choice of organisational structure again depends on cultural, political and other constraints; and implementing the most appropriate structure may not be possible.

Case study | Eurostar project

An example of a large, complex, and politically constrained, engineering project was the development of the Eurostar train that runs through the Channel Tunnel, providing direct services between London and Paris or Brussels plus links to many other European destinations (Figure 26).

Figure 26 Trans Manche Super Train *Eurostar* provides direct services between London and Paris or Brussels through the Channel Tunnel in under three hours at a maximum speed of 300km/h Source: Eurostar

The organisation and management of this project has been studied in detail by Bettina von Stamm and Max Boisot (von Stamm and Boisot, 1996; Boisot and von Stamm, 1996). They argue that the complexity of such a project should be matched by the complexity of the organisational structure to manage and develop it. The complexity was measured in terms of the number of technical components and their interaction, the degree of innovation, the time available to complete it, and the number of organisations and national cultures involved in the project.

So a highly complex international project, such as the Eurostar train, indicates an organisational structure such as a strong matrix. A strong matrix allows a high degree of cooperation and coordination between the many participants involved in the development.

The Eurostar project involved French, British and Belgian national railways, a consortium of four French, four British and two Belgian train manufacturers and their main suppliers, plus French, British and Belgian consultancies to design the exterior and interiors of the train. The sheer number of organisations and their different cultures provided one major element of complexity.

Another element of complexity was the degree of technical innovation involved. However, because the train was perceived as an incrementally improved version of the French high-speed train, the TGV (*Train à grande vitesse*), this complexity was not appreciated at first. It emerged that, while the mechanical systems were largely based on the TGV-*Atlantique,* the *Eurostar* involved highly complex and innovative technical design of the electrical and electronic control systems. This was due to the fact that the train had to cope with four different power supply and signalling systems. It also had to meet the safety regulations of three countries, plus those of the Channel Tunnel, and run through the smaller tunnels and platforms on the British side of the Channel.

The largely functional type of organisation set up to manage this project was not well suited to cope with all this complexity. One consequence was that completion of the project was delayed by 18 months and cost considerably more than planned. Basically, the organisation comprised two coordinating groups through which all decisions were routed. These were the International Project Group (IPG) comprising three senior engineers representing the customer railways plus an administrator, and the Trans Manche Super Train Group (TMSTG) headed by a project manager. Both the IPG and the TMSTG project managers had a high-level group overseeing their progress.

These three bodies coordinated the work of a series of working groups within the manufacturing consortium that developed the train, plus the input of the design consultancies (Figure 27). No direct contact was possible between the manufacturers responsible for developing a component and any of the customer railways. All enquiries had to be passed up the lines of command within the manufacturing consortium, sanctioned by the project manager of the TMSTG as well as the IPG, then to be passed down again along the lines of responsibility within each railway.

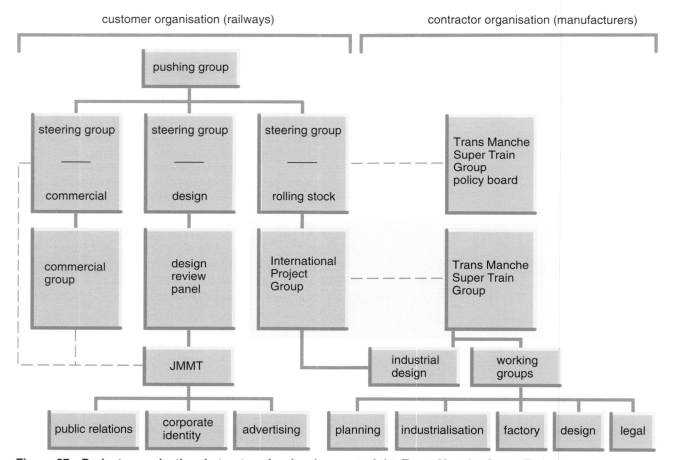

Figure 27   Project organisational structure for development of the Trans Manche Super Train *Eurostar*
Source: Boisot and von Stamm, 1996, p. 12

Although this organisational structure was supposed to facilitate cooperation and coordination, in practice each country's manufacturers and design consultancies worked fairly independently on the tasks they had been allocated. Communication was often difficult and inadequate, and so their work had to be integrated as best it could in the final design of the train. The interior of the train, for example, ended up looking to some eyes as if it had been created by designers from three different countries (as it had) rather than as a coordinated whole. (In 2003 the interiors were redesigned with help from the famous French designer, Philippe Starck.) Von Stamm and Boisot observe that, given all this, delivery of the Eurostar trains with a delay of just 18 months was a major achievement. But this was more due to the high level of commitment and effort of all parties to the project, and the hard work and skill of the TMSTG project managers appointed at the later stages, rather than the most appropriate organisational structure. This should have been a matrix-type organisation that would have established a project team headed by a strong project manager who would be allowed direct communication to the various representatives of the railways and the manufacturers. Boisot and Stamm comment that:

> The Eurostar's project organisation had a strong functional flavour to it. Within the project structure, the IPG and [the] TMSTG project manager assumed the role of project integrators. Cross-functional integration thus took place at the highest level. While the project's complexity called for a highly flexible organisation, the functionally oriented structure that was used – in combination with geographical distance and language problems – made communication very difficult. The project would have benefited from a matrix structure that facilitated negotiation and adjustments to unforeseen developments ... instead of responding to the coordination problem by creating an integrated collocated project team, project participants did the opposite. Matters were dealt with piecemeal ... and then presented the other parties as a *fait accompli*...

> In the course of the project participants gradually came to realise that its complexity was greater than originally anticipated, and the skills and organisation required for the development of Eurostar might differ after all from those needed to incrementally improve a TGV. Yet the project organisation ... remained fixed throughout ... the form used was better adapted to the needs of routine production, i.e. of just another batch of TGVs – than of a one-off engineering project. Had the project's full complexity been realised from the outset, a more sophisticated organisation response would have been possible. [...] If objective task complexity is irreducible then ... the appropriate organisational response has to be a move... towards a more matrix-like structure. Only then will task and organisational response be in balance. This did not happen.

> (Boisot and von Stamm, 1996, pp. 27–9)

It seems the Eurostar project succeeded largely *despite* the project's largely functional-type organisation than because of it. This was fortunate because, as Boisot and von Stamm observe, with so many participants from three countries involved, 'for political reasons' a matrix structure 'was never an option for the Eurostar project'. Another factor was that a matrix organisation could itself have added further complexity to the already complicated task of coordinating the activities of the many participants. In other words, which organisational structure is adopted to manage a project depends on what can be done in practice as well as what is best in theory.

In the case of the *Eurostar* a strong matrix organisational structure would probably have been the best option. But in practice because of the number of participants from three different countries involved this may not have been possible, even if the actual complexity of the project had been appreciated at the start.

SAQ 4

What organisational structure would you choose for (a) the design of an innovative consumer product and (b) a large-scale engineering project involving technical innovation? Give reasons for your choice.

Key points of Section 3

- Concurrent, simultaneous or phase overlapping, cross-functional ('rugby team') approaches enable NPD projects to be carried out more quickly and efficiently than traditional linear ('relay race') or iterative ('volleyball') approaches.

- The inputs from different functions to an NPD project can be organised in various ways – via separate functional departments; by establishing a dedicated project team; via a strong matrix structure under a 'heavyweight' project manager; or a weak matrix under a 'lightweight' project manager.

- Functional organisational structures foster deep disciplinary specialisation, but are generally ill suited to innovative NPD projects. Project teams are good for innovative projects, but may pose problems of accessing and maintaining specialist expertise. Matrix organisations are an attempt to obtain the advantages of both functional and project organisations, but involve more administrative and management effort.

- NPD projects usually involve inputs from a network of suppliers and/or partner companies as well as from the functions within a company.

- Communication and coordination between NPD team members and departments may be facilitated by collocation in a shared workspace and by providing an informal and relaxed work environment, and/or via computing and communications technologies.

- Computing systems to aid NPD include tools for: project planning and control; information storage and retrieval; communications; computer-aided design, simulation and rapid prototyping.

- Companies can adopt appropriate structures for innovative NPD projects, but this often involves difficult organisational change and may not be possible due to cultural, political or other constraints.

4 Strategies for new product development

The Garden Vac case study showed that an important element in its successful development by Flymo was how well the innovation fitted the strategy of the company that took it on. Recall how the Electrolux Floor-care division eventually decided a garden vacuuming product did not fit into its product range, and so the prototype was passed to the Flymo part of the Electrolux group. Flymo was looking for a garden tidy product to extend its range and its seasonal garden equipment sales period into the autumn.

As part of its strategic product planning Flymo had to decide whether to import one of the existing American 'blowervac' products, develop an improved version of a US product to overcome their drawback of clogging by wet leaves, or develop its own new product. John Coathupe's invention offered Flymo the opportunity to license, develop and be first to market with a 'new-to-the-world' product.

In the *Invention and innovation* block you were introduced to the idea that invention and innovation can be driven by what was called 'business strategy'. I'll look at this in a bit more detail by examining how the business strategy model (Figure 28) of the whole Electrolux group influences its NPD activities (as discussed in Jerrard et al, 2002).

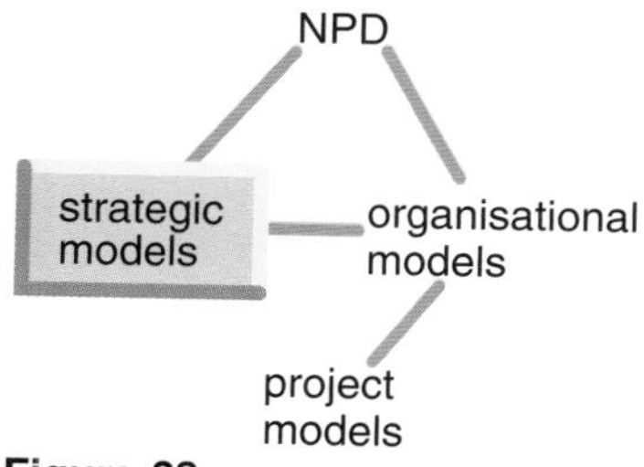

Figure 28

Case study Electrolux group – business strategy

The Electrolux group is the world's largest manufacturer of refrigerators, cookers, washing machines, chainsaws and lawnmowers. Its business strategy arises from the visions and values of the group, including its long-standing environmental policy; the evolving needs of its domestic and professional customers; and the changing business environment, especially the actions of its competitors and suppliers.

As part of its business strategy, the group restructured in 1997 and 2000. Electrolux sold its industrial products, sewing machines, agricultural implements and several other businesses acquired since 1925, to focus on its well-known indoor and outdoor consumer durables brands, such as AEG, Electrolux, Frigidaire, Zanussi and Flymo, and professional products such as laundry equipment and chainsaws. Electrolux's business strategy has three elements.

1 *Technology strategy.* This aims to ensure the company is keeping abreast of, and carrying out its own, R&D on technologies relevant to its business now and in the future.

2 *Market strategy.* This involves understanding how markets, society, the competition and legislation are evolving and deciding which markets and market segments the company should focus on, now and in the future.

3 *Product strategy.* This concerns which product classes, product families and products the company should develop, make and sell.

Electrolux's integrated product development process (IPDP) is guided by these three strategies. Integrated product development is a team-based approach that considers product design, process technology and market requirements throughout product development. The IPDP provides the link between Electrolux's long-term strategies and its current NPD projects (Figure 29a).

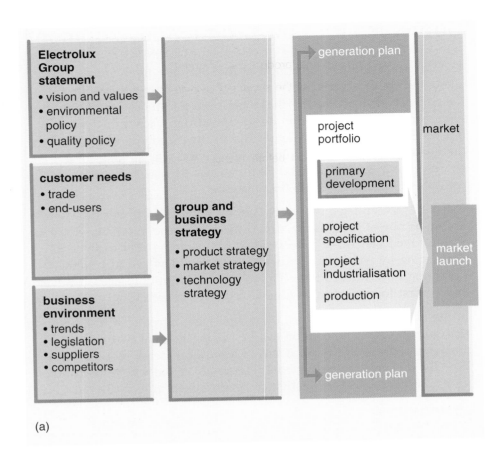

(a)

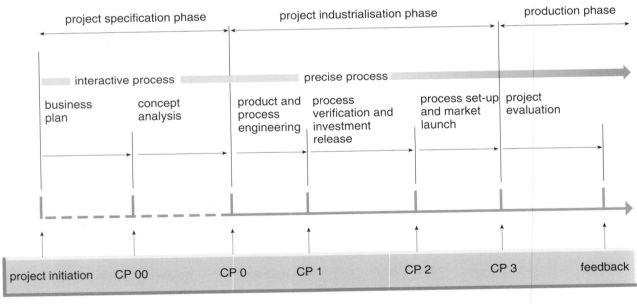

(b)

Figure 29 (a) Electrolux's integrated product development process and its relation to business strategy; (b) Electrolux's integrated product development process for an individual project. Sources: (a and b) adapted from *Electrolux IPDP Manual*, 1994 and 1997, by Jerrard et al, 2002, pp. 14, 19

Within this strategic framework, Electrolux plans the portfolio of projects it wishes to undertake and carries out two types of development project: 'primary development' and 'product development':

> Primary development is the systematic testing of new technologies, marketing concepts or production methods for the eventual creation of new or next generation products, production processes and marketing. The purpose of primary development is to reduce uncertainties concerning technologies, customer demands, feasibility, time and cost before product development projects are started.
>
> (*Electrolux IPDP Manual*, 1994, 1997, quoted in Jerrard et al, 2002, p. 16)

Primary development prepares Electrolux for the creation of future product families and the incorporation of new technological features into its existing products. All outcomes of primary development projects, such as concept designs and prototypes of possible future products, new components or production processes, are stored for later use in a 'primary development bank'.

Like primary development projects, product development projects arise from the group's strategies. Product development projects can draw on ideas and hardware from the primary development bank. However, rather than the open, exploratory nature of primary development, product development follows a structured process (similar to the stage-gate process outlined in Section 2) in which senior managers have to sign off at several checkpoints that the project has met given technical, market and financial criteria (Figure 29b).

This integrated product development process has three phases.

1   *Project specification*. Market and business analyses are carried out, project organisation, time and budget are set, a patent search is made and product concepts are explored to the working prototype stage. Concept design takes into account manufacturing and the use of key suppliers. An environmental assessment is an important part of the specification phase. This work leads to CP 0 (checkpoint zero), the critical decision whether to invest the large sums required for detailed development and manufacture (industrialisation) of the product. At CP 0 considerable work has been carried out to ensure the project is aligned with the strategies of the company before the final decision to invest is made.

2   *Project industrialisation*. The prototype product is designed in detail and tested, manufacturing processes are engineered and installed, agreements with key suppliers and market launch plans are made, and instructions, sales and service material is prepared. To get to through this phase the project has to pass through three checkpoints (CP 1 to CP 3).

3   *Production*. The project is evaluated using early market and other feedback, which if satisfactory leads to the ramp-up to full production.

Jerrard et al (2002, p. 20) conclude that:

> Electrolux like any successful large manufacturer, has a well defined new product development process ... Within a single model of the design process, the company explicitly links company vision and values to business strategies and thence into products that embody them. The same model shows ... how many of these developments are outside the time constraints of normal NPD process, being held

in a primary development bank to await incorporation into products when the market is ... ready for them. Such sophisticated practices are more typical of the motor car industry than domestic consumer products.

Like Electrolux, the Royal Philips Electronics group also plans a portfolio of new products for the short, medium and long term guided by the company's mission (including its sustainability policy discussed in Part 2) and its business strategy (Muller, 2004). To aid product planning Philips has carried out a number of so-called 'roadmap' studies to explore the evolution of markets, technologies and the business environment and to identify emerging needs, future opportunities and the technologies the company should invest in to enable it to develop new products and systems for the future. Planned new products are then developed through Philips' concurrent, team-based product creation process (see Section 3, Figure 20).

The videos 'Philips: introduction' on the T211 DVD and 'Philips: new product development' on the T307 DVD show this multinational's strategic approach to product planning and development. If you haven't done so already, view these videos at a convenient point during your study of this section.

SAQ 5

Draw a table to show how the main phases and checkpoints of Electrolux's integrated product development process (Figure 29b) and Philips' product creation process (Figure 20) compare to Pugh's design process model and Cooper's stage-gate model outlined in Section 2 of this block.

How do the idealised models and the use of NPD teams discussed in Section 3 compare with recommended practice at Electrolux and Philips?

Exercise 4   Strategic NPD approaches

When you have viewed the *Philips: New product development* video on the T307 DVD, plus its associated course team comments, compare the approaches to strategic product planning at Electrolux and Philips. Allow about 20 minutes for this exercise, before looking at the discussion below.

Discussion

I've compared Electrolux's and Philips' approaches to product planning and how they relate to their business strategies in the table below. Philips takes a longer-term and more future-oriented approach to R&D and product planning than Electrolux. In particular, Philips uses strategic design teams to generate new product and business concepts that may then be developed by the company's research departments and product divisions. This is probably because Philips mainly produces electronic products, while Electrolux focuses on domestic appliances and gardening equipment that have less potential for radical innovation. Both companies use long-established environmental or sustainability policies to help guide their strategy and NPD projects.

Electrolux	Philips
vision and values environmental policy business strategy	vision and mission sustainability policy company strategy roadmaps
Primary development: R&D, concept designs and prototypes of possible future products, new components or production processes. Stored in a 'primary development bank'.	*Horizon 3*: strategic design thinking on visions for society, design and technology up to 20 years ahead. Long-term R&D projects. Concepts and prototypes of products for possible future development.
	Horizon 2: identifying new product or business opportunities 3–7 years ahead and investing in realising those opportunities. Medium-term R&D projects.
Product development: planning development and launch of individual and families of new products. May draw on ideas and technologies from the primary development bank.	*Horizon 1*: planning and development of new and improved products and product families for manufacture 1–5 years ahead.

4.1 Competitive strategies

Product development driven by long-term technology, market and product strategies, and supported by in-house R&D is only practical for very large businesses, such as Electrolux and Philips. Small and medium-sized companies need a simpler approach to strategic planning of NPD projects.

Here I'll focus on competitive strategies that are, in principle, available to any company, or even to an individual inventor, designer or entrepreneur.

Several classifications have been proposed for 'competitive' or 'innovation' strategies.

Probably the best-known classification is Michael Porter's (1990, p. 37). He identified two basic competitive strategies.

- *Lower cost.* The ability of a company to design, produce and market comparable products more efficiently than its competitors.

- *Differentiation.* The ability to provide products that offer unique and superior value to the buyer in terms of quality, special features, or after sale service.

A company may focus on either of these two strategies to guide its new product (and manufacturing process) development projects. Dyson Ltd, for example, has focused firmly on differentiation of its cleaners and washing machines from the competition through technology and design. But a company will often produce a range of products based on a mix of these two strategies. For example, it may design basic products for the low-priced segment of the market and higher-specification products for customers wanting higher quality and more design features. In fact, to succeed in today's highly competitive markets, it's often necessary for new products to be both lower cost *and* differentiated.

Porter's classification, however, is too broad to cover all the available competitive or innovation strategies. A long-established, more detailed classification scheme is that by Ansoff and Stewart (1967), which builds on the scheme you met in the *Invention and innovation* block.

Ansoff and Stewart identified four competitive strategies for a technology-based business.

1 *First to market*. This strategy aims to be first to introduce an innovative, new-to-the-world product onto the market. It is the most aggressive strategy of the four because it risks large investments in R&D, design, manufacturing and marketing that only return a profit if and when the innovation sells in sufficient volume. It is usually based on a strong research programme, technological or design leadership, and good protection of intellectual property. Although risky, it is potentially the most rewarding because it gives the company a 'head start' over the competition.

This lead can then be maintained by a stream of incremental improvements to the original innovation. Successful examples include the innovation of the audio CD by Sony and Philips, Dyson's original cyclonic vacuum cleaner and new designs such as The Ball tilting and pivoting cleaner that followed it (Figure 30); and Apple's iPod digital music players, iTunes software and online music store.

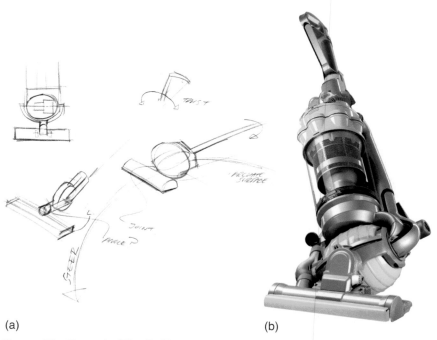

(a)   (b)

Figure 30   Dyson's 'The Ball' cyclonic cleaner launched in 2005 tilts and pivots around a ball containing the motor for greater manoeuvrability: (a) initial concept sketch; (b) final product Sources: (a and b) Dyson Ltd
Innovative designs such as this, using Dyson's patented cyclonic technology, are developed to keep Dyson ahead of the growing competition in bagless cleaners that use different collection systems

2 *Follow the leader*. This strategy aims to develop a product similar to a potentially successful product in the market, as rapidly as possible. This strategy is based on a strong development capability and the right balance of strength between the technological, marketing and manufacturing functions so that the company can respond effectively and quickly as the market starts its growth phase.

A company using this strategy benefits by learning from any mistakes made by the first-to-market innovator. The strategy can be highly rewarding, but the company needs to deal with the innovator's intellectual property rights and risks being overtaken by rival companies. Example products include the various bagless cleaners developed by Electrolux (Figure 31) and other appliance manufacturers after the Dyson cleaner had captured a large market share.

3 *Me-too*. This strategy aims to develop a product that has a new design and/or a lower price in a mature market. It is based on superior manufacturing efficiency and cost control. Consequently it needs strong manufacturing and product design functions in order to copy new designs quickly and modify them for reduced costs and special features. It avoids the risk of expensive R&D, but has the corresponding risk of falling behind new technology. Examples include the many designs of audio CD and digital music players produced by different manufacturers.

4 *Application engineering*. This strategy aims to develop products to fit the needs of particular customers in a mature market. Consequently it requires technically perceptive salesmen and sales engineers who work closely with customers and/or product designers. It needs a flair for minimising development and manufacturing costs, for example by using the same 'platform' of subsystems and components in different applications to produce a variety of products for different customer requirements. Car manufacturers often employ this strategy when developing updated models or additions to their range.

More recently, Ulrich and Eppinger (2000, p. 41) have identified a similar set of strategies, which they call technology leadership; imitative; cost leadership; and customer focus.

Many companies compete through more than one of these strategies and plan their portfolio of new products accordingly. For example, a company may plan over the next five years to develop one new 'first to market' product and a family of 'application engineering' variants of existing products.

Of course, not all businesses have the resources to choose between all four strategies. Individual innovators and small companies may only be able to follow either a 'first to market' strategy with an innovative niche product or a 'me too' strategy with an incremental improvement to an existing design.

Figure 31 Electrolux Cyclone Power Max Z5500 cyclonic cleaner Source: Electrolux

4.2 S-curves and disruptive innovations

One issue that faces companies competing in markets affected by rapid technological change is which technologies to base their products on. Identifying scientific and technological developments and trends is an important part of strategic product planning. One method some planners use for analysing technological trends is the s-curve, which plots a single measure of the performance – for example speed, power, reliability – of a class of products based on a particular technology either against time or (as originally formulated by Foster, 1988) against the R&D effort required to improve that performance.

s-curve

s-shaped graph of the improvement in performance of a new product when plotted against time or development effort

The s-curve shows that for most innovations performance improves slowly at first, accelerates and then levels off (Figure 32). Products based on a new technology then can catch up and overtake the performance of products based on the established technology. The established products, and the companies that make them, are then vulnerable to being displaced by the products and companies using the new technology.

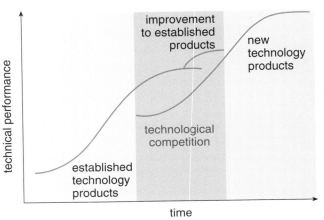

Figure 32 Typical s-curves for an established and a new technology. As the performance of products based on the established technology levels off, they face serious competition from products based on the new technology. In response, the established technology products may be improved further, but eventually they are still overtaken in performance by the new technology products. Source: based on Foster, 1988, p. 102 and Open University, 1996, pp. 83–5

S-curves are discussed further in the *Diffusion* block, but I introduce them here because of their relevance to a company's technology strategy and product planning.

The question for companies making products based on an established technology is whether to make a strategic switch to a new technology and, if so, when. Often, companies fail to make the switch and instead focus either on trying to improve the performance of products based on the established technology (and/or on increasing their sales and marketing efforts). This strategy can work for a time, and indeed start the performance s-curve for the established technology to rise again (see Figure 32). But often the new technology cannot be out-performed and either the companies are forced to adopt it using a 'me too' strategy or they go out of business.

Earlier you saw that attempts to improve the performance of an established technology and class of product – helping to sustain the companies and industries that produce it – are called sustaining innovations. Disruptive innovations are the new technologies adopted by competing companies that may displace, or even destroy, those established firms and industries.

For example, the chemical film manufacture Kodak realised its survival was threatened unless it changed its technology strategy and product portfolio to meet the competition from 'disruptive' digital photography. Kodak therefore put great effort into developing a range of easy-to-use digital cameras plus ink-jet printers, software and paper (Figure 33). With digital technology in place, Kodak ceased to market conventional film cameras in European and US markets in 2004.

Figure 33   Kodak EasyShare digital photo printer with a camera docked Source: Kodak Ltd

Case study   Excavator technology

If a company is faced with products based on a new technology produced by rival enterprises, it has to decide whether to try to meet or to ignore the challenge. Such a situation arose when manufacturers of cable-operated excavators found hydraulic backhoe excavators pioneered by a British company, JCB, entering the market in the early 1950s (as was described in Section 2).

Most established cable-operated excavator manufacturers ignored the disruptive hydraulic technology, which initially had much less capacity and reach than their cable-operated products, but were suited to small excavating tasks such as laying water pipes and digging house foundations. But as the hydraulic technology improved in capacity, most cable excavator manufacturers were put out of business or forced into specialist markets for large-scale mining and dredging equipment (Christensen, 2003, p. 72–3).

SAQ 6

What competitive strategy did Flymo pursue to compete in the garden products market with the Garden Vac? What response did Black & Decker adopt after Flymo had successfully launched the Garden Vac?

SAQ 7

Using Porter's competitive strategies, what do technical innovation and product design offer in helping a company to gain a competitive advantage? Give one or more examples to illustrate your answer.

Key points of Section 4

- NPD projects should only be planned and carried out that support a company's business strategy. This business strategy derives from a company's vision and may be elaborated into technology, market and product strategies.

- Multinational companies, like Electrolux and Philips, may engage in planning for a portfolio of short-, medium- and long-term NPD projects supported by strategic design and R&D.

- Companies of all sizes – as well as individual inventors, designers and entrepreneurs – may adopt one or more competitive strategies to guide their product planning and development. These include: Porter's lower cost and/or differentiation strategies; and/or Ansoff and Stewarts's first to market, follow the leader, me too or application engineering strategies. Which is best suited to a particular company, or individual innovator, depends on their capabilities.

- Established companies need to keep abreast of new technologies that may affect their products and respond to competition from rival companies that have adopted new technology. If they focus just on 'sustaining' innovation, established companies, and even whole industries, may eventually be forced out of business by 'disruptive' innovation.

Part 2
Product development and the
environment

5 Environmental context

In Part 1, I discussed the activity and management of new product development (NPD) at project, organisational and strategic levels. In Part 2, I'm going to discuss how environmental issues are having an increasing influence on NPD at these three levels. This time, I'm going to start at the strategic, and then the organisational and project levels, of designing individual products for reduced environmental impacts, including some specific ecodesign tools. I'll finish by moving back up to the strategic level to consider the potential for designing systems of products and services with much lower environmental impacts than is possible by ecodesigning individual products.

SAQ 8

What are the links between the project, organisational and strategic levels of NPD introduced in Part 1? Spend five minutes on this question before looking at my answer at the end of the block.

Before I discuss the effects of environmental issues on NPD, I'll consider how and why those issues have increasingly influenced individuals, industry and governments. This means a brief review of the effects of industrialisation on the environment, as outlined below.

5.1 Environmental issues

Concern about the environmental impacts of industrialisation has a long history. Industrialisation involves a growing economy based on the production and consumption of an increasing volume and variety of products and services. An industrial economy and consumer society therefore involve an increasing demand for energy, materials and chemicals with the resultant consequences of environmental pollution, resource depletion, land-take and waste. Starting in the early twentieth century, environmental concern focused initially on the impacts of the industrial economy on wildlife and landscapes.

Contemporary environmental concern stems from the 1950s and 1960s after a number of major environmental problems had reached wide public and political attention. These included deaths and disease in the UK from smog; contamination of the seas and coastline from a major oil spill off Cornwall and from mercury pollution in Japan; and the effects of DDT and other chemical pesticides on human health and wildlife in the US. Concern about environmental issues reached crisis proportions in the 1970s with the 1972 Club of Rome report, *The Limits to Growth* (Meadows, 1974), which warned of long-term catastrophic ecological effects of exponential economic growth. In the shorter term the focus was on the energy problem raised by a four-fold increase in oil prices in 1973–74.

Further major environmental accidents and problems emerged during the 1970s and into the 1980s. These included: further large oil spills from tankers; the death of millions of trees due to acid rain; toxic pollution from chemical production; the near meltdown of the US nuclear power plant at Three Mile Island in 1979; the hole in the ozone layer due to emissions of chlorofluorocarbon gases (CFCs) into the upper atmosphere; and radiation exposure from the explosion and fire at the Chernobyl nuclear reactor in Russia in 1986 (Elliott, 1997).

In response, legislation to control pollution and international agreements, notably the 1987 Montreal Protocol to phase out CFCs and other ozone-depleting substances, were attempts to deal with such environmental problems. Another response was a series of international conferences, starting with the United Nations Conference on the Human Environment held in Stockholm in 1972.

5.1.1 Sustainable development

The 1972 Stockholm conference was the first major international meeting having the word 'environment' in its title and the first international attempt to explore connections between environmental protection and social and economic development. It debated how the demand by developing countries for economic development to lift their populations out of poverty could be met without destroying the planet, given that the industrialised world was already consuming most of the world's energy and resources. (This issue is discussed further in the *Consumption* block.)

Since then, there have been global UN conferences on environment and development at Rio de Janeiro in 1992 and Johannesburg in 2002 as well as numerous books, reports and meetings discussing environmental problems and the issue of environment and development. Notable among these was the Brundtland Commission's report titled *Our Common Future* (World Commission on Environment and Development, 1987), which popularised the term sustainable development.

sustainable development

economic and social development consistent with long term environmental sustainability

The Brundtland Commission's definition of sustainable development as 'development which meets the needs of the present without compromising the ability of future generations to meet their needs' is the most widely used; you met it in the *Invention and innovation* block. But there are many other definitions. For example, the European Commission's definition includes the following economic, social and environmental (as well as a further two political) elements:

1   balanced and equitable economic development

2   high levels of employment, social cohesion and inclusiveness

3   a high level of environmental protection and responsible use of natural resources.

(http://europa.eu.int/comm/sustainable/pages/idea_en.htm [accessed 17.3.06])

The UK has similar sustainable development objectives that are summarised in Box 3.

Box 3   Sustainable development principles

The goal of sustainable development is to enable all people throughout the world to satisfy their basic needs and enjoy a better quality of life, without compromising the quality of life of future generations.[...] The following is the set of shared UK principles that we will use to achieve our sustainable development purpose.

Living within environmental limits

Respecting the limits of the planet's environment, resources and biodiversity – to ... ensure that the natural resources needed for life are unimpaired and remain so for future generations.

Ensuring a strong, healthy and just society

Meeting the diverse needs of all people in existing and future communities... and creating equal opportunity for all.

Achieving a sustainable economy

Building a strong, stable and sustainable economy which provides prosperity and opportunities for all [...]

Using sound science responsibly

Ensuring policy is developed and implemented on the basis of strong scientific evidence [...]

Promoting good governance

Actively promoting effective, participative systems of governance in all levels of society [...]

(DEFRA, 2005, p. 16)

So, sustainable development means more than preserving resources and the natural environment for current and future generations. Sustainable development is concerned with the social and economic development of the world's population to ensure a decent standard of living and quality of life for those in the developing as well as the industrialised world. Sustainable development is said to rest on three pillars of sustainability – *social*, *economic*, and *environmental*. But in this course the team would argue that social and economic sustainability is not possible without a sustainable natural environment. In addition, the drive for social and economic sustainability for the developing world, because it involves increased production and consumption, can conflict with, and so must be balanced against, environmental sustainability.

Hence, the main concern in this course is with the environmental aspects of sustainable development, in particular considering the environmental impacts of product development and innovation. Therefore, as the UK government sustainable development strategy observed:

> The past 20 years have seen a growing realisation that the current model of development is unsustainable. On the one hand we see the increasing burden our way of life places on the planet [...] On

the other hand we see a world where over a billion people live on less than a dollar a day [...] sustainable poverty eradication depends on the poor having access to adequate natural resources and a healthy environment. Unless we start to make real progress toward reconciling these contradictions, we ... face a future that is less certain and less secure than we in the UK have enjoyed over the past fifty years. We need to make a decisive move towards more sustainable development both because it is the right thing to do, and because it is in our long-term best interests.

(DEFRA, 2005, p. 12)

Of the many environmental issues, probably the most important to emerge is the impact on the global climate of the emissions of greenhouse gases, especially carbon dioxide, from the burning of fossil fuels. Fossil fuels are used in ever-increasing amounts to generate electricity, to heat or cool buildings, to power cars, trucks and other vehicles, and to produce and operate all the products and services consumed by the world's population, mainly in the industrialised countries.

As a result, in 2005 under the Kyoto Protocol, the targets agreed to reduce their greenhouse gas emissions came into force in most industrialised countries – with the notable exception of the USA, the largest consumer of fossil fuels. The UK government set itself more ambitious targets than required by the Protocol, aiming to reduce UK CO_2 emissions by 20% from their 1990 levels by 2010 and by 60% by 2050. Such reductions in emissions are of the order that international scientific opinion considers necessary to stabilise concentrations of CO_2 in the atmosphere in order to tackle climate change.

Of course, climate change is only one of many issues that affect the natural environment. Environmental issues range from local problems, such as litter, vehicle noise and localised pollution; regional issues such as waste disposal and threats to human health or wildlife associated with toxic substances; to global impacts such as depletion of key material resources, and the hole in the ozone layer. The global problems can of course have local and regional impacts.

5.2 Role of design and innovation

While most of these environmental issues arise from industrialisation and the consumer society in general, not all are directly connected to the design, development, manufacture and use of individual products. However, many are due to products. For example, Figure 34 shows some of the environmental impacts of the manufacture, use and disposal of a refrigerator, including resource depletion, climate change, air and water pollution, land degradation, waste, and effects on wildlife biodiversity. Previously, ozone depletion from the release of CFC or hydrochlorofluorocarbon (HCFC) refrigerants and insulation blowing agents into the upper atmosphere would also have been included. However, these chemicals have now mainly been replaced due to the Montreal Protocol plus campaigns, and research and development into the use of hydrocarbons as alternatives.

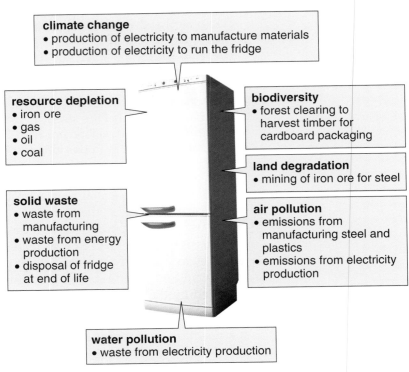

climate change
- production of electricity to manufacture materials
- production of electricity to run the fridge

resource depletion
- iron ore
- gas
- oil
- coal

solid waste
- waste from manufacturing
- waste from energy production
- disposal of fridge at end of life

biodiversity
- forest clearing to harvest timber for cardboard packaging

land degradation
- mining of iron ore for steel

air pollution
- emissions from manufacturing steel and plastics
- emissions from electricity production

water pollution
- waste from electricity production

Figure 34 Environmental impacts of a refrigerator Source: adapted from Lewis et al, 2001, p.101; photo from Alamy Images

The role of design and technology in both creating environmental problems and in helping to move towards social, economic and environmental sustainability has long been recognised.

The British Arts and Crafts movement of the late nineteenth century criticised the factory-made goods and pollution of the Industrial Revolution and advocated a revival of handicrafts, a return to a simpler way of life and an improvement in the design of domestic objects. One of the movement's founders, William Morris, put the ideas into practice by setting up a company to design and produce furniture, textiles and wallpaper using traditional craft methods. The movement was influential among progressive artists, designers, architects, retailers and manufactures, and spread across Europe and America in the period up to the First World War (V & A, 2005).

Although the products of the Arts and Crafts movement reached relatively few people, it helped lay the foundations for the modernist movement in architecture and design originating in Germany in the 1920s, with its concern for economy of materials and fitness for purpose in buildings and mass-produced products. In America, also starting in the 1920s, Buckminster Fuller created his radical designs of buildings and vehicles that gave maximum human benefit from minimal use of energy and materials. His design principle of 'doing more from less', exemplified in his geodesic dome buildings, had a great influence on generations of designers and architects.

Arising out of the 1960s counter-culture and the environmental concerns of the 1970s, the alternative technology movement, and books by its proponents such as *Radical Technology* (Boyle and Harper, 1976), were highly critical of the existing technological, social and economic system. Alternative technologists proposed designs and innovations, from autonomous housing independent of central sources of energy, water and food, to low-cost technologies for developing countries intended to meet environmental, social and human needs better than the products of the dominant system. A parallel movement for socially responsible design, notably put forward in *Design for the Real World* by Victor Papanek (1971, 1984), criticised the use of design by industry to create products that did not meet genuine social needs, and advocated the redirection of industrial design to meet the needs of the disabled, the developing world and the environment.

Although governments and industry may not agree with the social and political agendas of these various radical movements, the ideas about ecological design and innovation they pioneered have become almost mainstream. One sign of this was a manifesto from the leaders of over 50 multinational corporations presented at the 1992 UN Conference on Environment and Development (Schmidheiney, 1992), which argued that business had a critical role in sustainable development, combining economic growth with environmental protection by means of eco-efficient design and technical innovation.

In this part, I'll be examining how product design and technical innovation may be used to reduce environmental impacts and to help move towards a more sustainable future. The approaches range from incremental changes to existing product designs (green design) to radical concepts for innovative technologies and systems (sustainable innovation). As you'll see much of which is being done by government and business is towards the incremental end of the spectrum, although more radical ideas are increasingly being considered and implemented.

Key points of Section 5

- Attempts to address the environmental impacts of production and consumption have evolved over many years from protecting wildlife and reducing pollution to aiming for sustainable development.

- Sustainable development rests on three pillars – social progress, economic development and environmental protection. In the long-term, without a sustainable environment, social progress and economic development are unlikely to be achieved.

- Radical ideas about ecological design and innovation have become almost mainstream as their role in attempts to reach environmental sustainability are being recognised.

Strategic responses to the environment

In the previous section, I briefly summarised the context in which today's environmental problems arose plus some historic responses to those problems. In this section, I'll examine how modern business is responding to key environmental issues, especially where they affect new product development and manufacture.

6.1 Environmental influences on NPD

A number of factors, or drivers, have shaped the growing recognition by designers, engineers and business managers of the need to address environmental issues in product development and manufacture.

The main *external* drivers are:

- *Environmental regulation, standards and voluntary agreements.* Increasingly tough legislation, both existing and anticipated, is an especially important driver because companies that fail to prepare for, and comply with, environmental laws face prosecution. Some important EU environmental legislation relevant to design and manufacture is outlined in Box 4 below.

- *Pressure from others in the supply chain.* This occurs when retailers, wholesalers or other manufacturers specify or wish to source greener products, materials or components.

- *Introduction of green products by competitors.* This is a response by competing businesses to actual or potential market demand.

- *Innovations in technology, materials, components and manufacturing processes.* These offer opportunities to reduce environmental impacts – for example, the development of products made from new lightweight, biodegradable or recycled materials.

- *Pressure from insurance companies, ethical investors and environmental groups.* Such pressure comes from requirements to tackle specific environmental issues, or to address sustainability more generally.

The main *internal* drivers are:

- *Market share.* The wish to gain a share of the green consumer market for environmentally friendly products.

- *Saving money.* The opportunity for significant cost savings from introducing more energy-efficient, less-wasteful and less-polluting manufacturing processes.

- *Commitment.* Management commitment to tackling environmental issues as an area of corporate social responsibility (CSR). This may be the result of their personal or company ethos, group headquarters' policy, or pressures from employees and shareholders.

corporate social responsibility

how businesses manage the economic, social, and environmental impacts of their operations to maximise the benefits and minimise the downsides

For example, Electrolux's business and product development strategy, (examined in Section 4) is guided by the group's environmental strategy. Electrolux's environmental strategy is, in turn, driven by society's response to environmental problems, ranging from local noise to global ozone depletion as reflected in environmental regulation, market demands for environmentally friendly products and pressures for resource and cost efficiency (Figure 35).

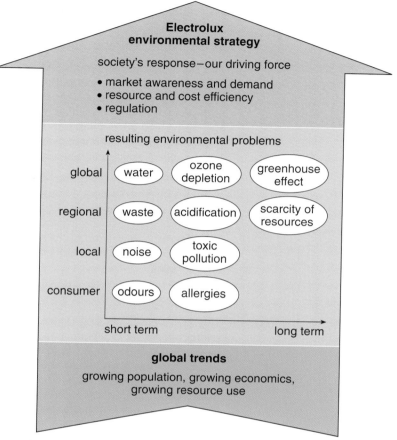

Figure 35 Sources and drivers for Electrolux's environmental strategy
Source: Electrolux

Box 4   Product-related environmental regulation

Much environmental regulation is concerned with controlling pollution from manufacture. However, there is an increasing amount of regulation – including legislation, voluntary agreements and standards – concerned with product design. The following is a small selection of relevant EU (European Union) and EC (European Commission) environmental directives and agreements and ISO (International Standards Organisation) standards.

Ecolabel

The EU ecolabel, first introduced in 1993 for washing machines and revised in 2000 to apply to a range of products from detergents to clothing, is a voluntary scheme designed to encourage businesses to market products that have lower environmental impacts over their life cycle. It also aims to enable European consumers to identify ecological products by the 'flower' symbol (see Figure 61).

Packaging Directive

The EC Packaging Directive, first introduced in 1994, aims to prevent the production of packaging waste, and reduce the amount of waste for final disposal through packaging reuse, recycling and other forms of recovery.

The directive sets requirements to be considered in packaging design and manufacture and toxic metal limits for packaging. A 2004 amendment increased the recycling targets for the Member States to be met by 2008, to 60% overall recovery of packaging waste; and 55% minimum and 80% maximum recycling of packaging waste.

Ecomanagement and Audit Scheme

The EU Ecomanagement and Audit Scheme (EMAS), introduced in 1995, is a voluntary management tool for companies and other organisations to evaluate, report and improve their environmental performance. It mainly concerns processes, but products may be included. Once an organisation has implemented an EMAS-approved environmental management system, an independent body audits the organisation's environmental work.

In 2001, EMAS was integrated with ISO 14001, the international standard for environmental management systems, published in 1996 by the International Standards Organisation. ISO 14001 is one of the ISO 14000 family of voluntary international standards concerning how an organisation is managed to minimise its harmful effects on the environment. The family also includes ISO 14062 on designing for the environment.

Energy Labelling Directive

The EC Energy Labelling Directive, introduced from 1996, required the energy efficiency of electrical appliances such as washing machines to be given a rating from A (up to A++ for refrigerators) to G displayed on an energy label for retailers and consumers (see Figure 62). For some products, the label provides other information such as performance and noise. Under the directive, there are regular reviews in which products that are more efficient are expected to be introduced and the least-efficient appliances withdrawn from the market.

End-of-Life Vehicle Directive

The EU End-of-Life Vehicle Directive (ELVD), introduced in 2003, aims to prevent waste from vehicles at the end of their lives and to increase the reuse, recycling and other forms of recovery of end-of-life vehicles (ELVs) and their components. It restricts the use of toxic metals in new vehicles, requires vehicle manufacturers to mark certain components to aid recovery and recycling and to provide information to facilitate dismantling.

extended producer responsibility

manufacturers take the main responsibility for the environmental impacts of products throughout their life cycle

The ELVD is an example of extended producer responsibility (EPR), the principle that manufacturers of products should take significant responsibility for the environmental impacts of their products throughout the product's entire life cycle.

Waste Electrical and Electronic Equipment Directive

The EC Waste Electrical and Electronic Equipment (WEEE) Directive implemented in 2006–7, aims to prevent the growing mountain of waste electrical and electronic equipment (WEEE, including appliances, electronic products, lighting and toys), and to increase their reuse, recycling and other forms of recovery (Figure 36). The directive encourages manufacturers to design electrical and electronic equipment to facilitate its dismantling and recovery, reuse and recycling. It requires manufacturers to arrange for WEEE to be collected and to inform consumers not to discard old products but to use the special facilities provided for recovery, reuse and recycling. WEEE is another example of extended producer responsibility.

Figure 36   The Royal Society of Arts' WEEE Man. A dramatic sculpture made from the 3.5 tonnes of waste electrical and electronic equipment (WEEE) a typical UK resident would produce in their lifetime, given present WEEE growth rates. Source: weeeman.org

Restriction of Hazardous Substances Directive

The EC Restriction of Hazardous Substances (RoHS) Directive introduced in 2006–7, in conjunction with WEEE, bans certain hazardous materials and chemicals such as lead, cadmium and mercury. These should not be used in the manufacture of electrical and electronic products, in order to protect human health and the environment in disposal and to facilitate waste recovery.

Batteries Directive

The EC Batteries Directive to be introduced in 2006, aims to maximise the collection and recycling of spent batteries and accumulators, and to reduce their disposal in the municipal waste stream. It sets eventual collection targets for spent portable batteries of 25% of annual sales, includes a partial ban on portable nickel–cadmium batteries, and bans disposal of vehicle batteries in landfill.

Directive on energy-using products

The EU directive on the ecodesign of energy-using products (EuPs) planned to come into force in 2006. The EuP Directive aims to encourage manufacturers to apply ecodesign (the integration of environmental considerations at the design phase) to minimise the environmental impacts of energy-using products over their life cycle. The impacts include consumption of energy, materials and natural resources, waste generation and release of greenhouse gases and hazardous substances. EuPs that have been awarded an EU ecolabel will be considered as having met the requirements of the directive.

Integrated product policy

EC Integrated product policy (IPP), due to be introduced after 2007. IPP seeks to minimise the environmental impacts of products by looking at all phases of their life cycle from 'cradle to grave' and taking action where it is most effective. IPP will involve a variety of tools – both voluntary and mandatory – including substance bans, voluntary agreements, environmental labelling and product design guidelines. Life cycle thinking, as required for IPP, will be introduced in Section 7.

Sources: http://www.dti.gov.uk/sustainability http://europa.eu.int/comm/environment (accessed 12.9.05)

6.2 From pollution control to designing for the environment

For many decades, the usual business responses to environmental issues were measures to reduce wastes and pollution *after* they had been produced; for example, by installing factory wastewater treatment plant or equipping cars with catalytic converters. However, from the late 1980s onwards some companies began to shift their attention from these end-of-pipe approaches towards developing cleaner production processes, which generate less pollution and waste in the first place, or make more efficient use of energy and materials.

end-of-pipe

technology used to treat, handle or dispose of emissions and wastes from production

cleaner production

reducing environmental impacts from processes by using better management strategies, methods and technologies

green products

products designed with the objective of reducing their impacts on the environment

Then, with the realisation that major environmental impacts can arise from materials choices and from the use and disposal of products, some companies' engineers and designers began to think in terms of designing green products. Green products are products designed with the objective of reducing their impact on the natural environment. The reduction is usually relative to a comparable existing product, hence the term 'greener product' is sometimes used instead.

The development of green(er) products in particular sectors has been greatly stimulated by environmental labelling. This includes the compulsory EU energy labelling of lighting and domestic appliances, but also voluntary environmental labels such as the Forest Stewardship Council (FSC) label on timber products and the EU ecolabel on paper products (see Box 4). The benefit of such labels has been to help retailers to source, or specify, greener products, and to stimulate competition among manufacturers to gain a good energy label rating, as well as to encourage consumers to buy green.

Businesses have therefore increasingly shifted their attention from trying to clean up a product's environmental impacts during its manufacture, use and disposal to designing out as many of the impacts as possible during product development. I'll discuss different strategic approaches to the design of green products – what is often termed designing for the environment (DfE) – in the next section.

Although there are some companies that specialise in developing and marketing green products – for example renewable energy devices, alternative fuel vehicles or clothes made from fairly traded, organic fibres – the majority of companies have had to introduce environmental factors into the design of their existing range of products. A good example is Black & Decker.

Case study   Black & Decker

Black & Decker is a global manufacturer of power tools, hardware and home improvement products such as the Mouse sander mentioned in Part 1. The company realised that it had to consider the environmental impacts of its products to compete with rival manufacturers like Bosch and to satisfy major retailers of its products, like B&Q. Other drivers for designing for the environment included compliance with legislation and the opportunities offered by new technologies (Figure 37). The company found that up to 80% of product costs and environmental impacts were determined at the design stage and that its different customers had different purchasing criteria – some prioritising performance and others energy consumption.

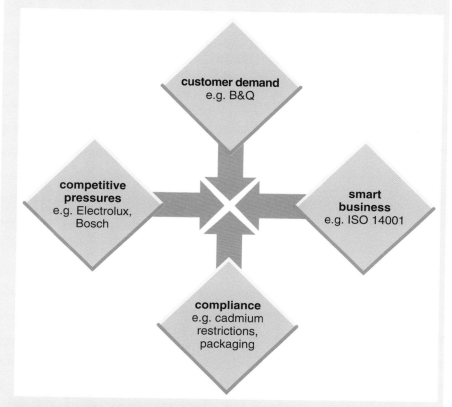

Figure 37   Black & Decker's assessment of drivers for design for the environment Source: Envirowise, p.9

Black & Decker therefore began a design for the environment (DfE) programme to identify opportunities to redesign its products to reduce both costs and environmental impacts, for example by elimination of hazardous materials and designing for ease of assembly and disassembly. The company now considers greener design as the 'smart thing' to do for legal, business and corporate responsibility reasons (Envirowise, 2001, pp. 9–11).

Of course, most companies don't have the resources of multinationals like Electrolux or Black & Decker to respond to environmental problems with comprehensive environmental strategies or DfE programmes. Instead, small- and medium-sized companies usually introduce cleaner production processes or develop greener products for strictly commercial reasons, such as maintaining or increasing their market share, and in order to comply with environmental legislation.

Neither do all companies make products sold directly to consumers. As you should recall from the *Markets* block, many companies are 'business to business' suppliers to other companies. For such suppliers the main environmental driver is the policy of their business customers. In particular, multinationals like Electrolux and major retailers like the DIY chain B&Q have been in the forefront of developing environmental and sustainability policies. This has had a trickledown effect on their supply chain whose members have to satisfy environmental or broader sustainability criteria in designing their products and components.

SAQ 9

Different EU and EC directives and regulations aim to reduce environmental impacts at different parts of a product's life cycle: from materials supply, through manufacture and use, to end-of-life recycling or disposal.

(a) Match the EU and EC directives in Box 4 to the most relevant parts of a product's life cycle.

(b) Which directives should be addressed during NPD?

(c) Which directives are examples of 'extended producer responsibility'?

SAQ 10

What were the main external and internal drivers that led Black & Decker to establish and undertake a design for the environment programme? Look back at the list of environmental drivers at the beginning of Section 6, the above Black & Decker case study and Figure 37.

Key points of Section 6

- Business response to environmental issues depends on a number of external and internal drivers, such as environmental legislation, market demands and opportunities, and corporate social responsibility.

- Business has shifted its emphasis in tackling environmental problems from end-of-pipe cleanup of product and manufacturing process impacts towards cleaner production processes and the design of greener products.

- New product development and manufacture is influenced by a number of EU and EC environmental directives and regulations.

Designing for the environment

7.1 Strategic approaches to DfE

In the previous section, I discussed the drivers that have led businesses to introduce design for the environment (DfE) programmes as part of their action on environmental issues, their environmental strategy or policy on sustainable development. In this and the next section, I'll examine four strategic approaches to designing for the environment available to designers, engineers, managers and policymakers.

green design

approach that reduces environmental impact but limited by focussing on one or two environmental objectives

1   Green design. With this approach products are developed so they have a reduced impact on the natural environment. However, this approach is limited by focusing on one or two environmental objectives when designing, redesigning or improving a product – for example conserving materials by manufacturing with recycled materials or conserving energy by increasing energy efficiency in use. Most existing environmental legislation attempts to encourage green design. It usually involves incremental innovation.

ecodesign

approach that reduces total environmental impact by considering a product's impact over its life cycle from 'cradle to grave'

2   Ecodesign. This approach is much more comprehensive than green design, because it attempts a balanced reduction in environmental impacts throughout the physical life cycle – from raw materials extraction to end-of-life disposal – when designing or redesigning a product. This approach is sometimes called life-cycle design. Some existing and proposed environmental legislation (such as IPP mentioned in Box 4) aims to encourage ecodesign. It may require architectural or modular innovation (as defined in Section 1).

sustainable design

radical approach for reducing environmental impact by using an alternative technical method to carry out the product's essential function. Often includes social and economic as well as environmental impacts

3   Sustainable design. This approach, instead of optimising the environmental impacts of an existing product through ecodesign, aims to fulfil the essential function of the product by using the least environmentally harmful technical solution. For example, instead of redesigning a boiler to be somewhat more efficient, the designer applies technology that is environmentally optimal such as solar energy to provide the essential function of providing household warmth. This approach is sometimes called green function innovation. It may involve radical technical innovation and often includes social and economic as well as environmental considerations – for example a product's fair trade implications, and the health and safety of the workers producing it.

sustainable innovation

radical approach for reducing environmental impact by considering a socio-technical systems intervention rather than by considering a product improvement

4   Sustainable innovation. This is even broader in scope than sustainable design, and goes beyond technical solutions. In this approach, new, environmentally optimal product–service mixes or systems are considered to provide a required function. For example, to provide the essential function of providing clean clothes, a sustainable innovation might involve establishing a network of community laundry services that use solar-heated water and collection and delivery booked by internet. This approach is sometimes called green system innovation. It is likely to involve socio-technical configurational innovation (as defined in Section 1) and includes social and economic as well as environmental considerations.

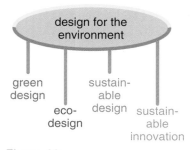

Figure 38

Figure 39 shows curves representing the four strategic DfE approaches with an indication of time-scale that each may require for implementation, plus its benefits in terms of increased 'eco-efficiency', and hence reduced environmental impacts. These eco-efficiency–time curves for different DfE approaches have some similarity to the performance–time s-curves for technologies introduced in Section 4.

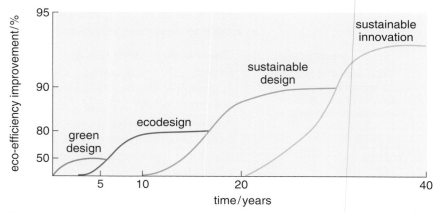

Figure 39   Four strategic approaches to designing for the environment
Source: adapted from Brezet, 1997, p. 22

Although the numbers are only approximate, Figure 39 indicates that green design may produce a 50 per cent (factor 2) improvement in eco-efficiency (i.e. halving energy and resource consumption) relative to existing products over five years. Ecodesign might produce an 80 per cent (factor 5) improvement within 10 years. Sustainable design and sustainable innovation may produce 90 per cent or more (factor 10 to 15) improvements in eco-efficiency compared to existing methods of supplying an essential function over time-periods of 20 to 35 years.

The idea of 'factor X' was popularised by von Weizsäcker et al (1997) in their book *Factor 4*. It refers to the reduction in energy and resource consumption for providing the equivalent function to that of an existing product by a more eco-efficient product or system. So a conventional refrigerator might be replaced by a super-insulated refrigerator with an efficient motor and compressor or a food preservation system based on new technology. Therefore, a factor 2 improvement in eco-efficiency means a product or system with a 50 per cent reduction in energy and resource consumption compared to existing products that offer the same function. Similarly, a factor 5 improvement means an 80 per cent reduction in energy and resource consumption.

> What percentage reduction in energy and resource consumption, and hence environmental impacts, is meant by a 'factor 10' improvement in eco-efficiency?
>
> Percentage reduction = (1 − 1/factor 10) x 100 = 90%.

eco-efficiency

reducing environmental impacts by technical rather than behavioural changes

More generally, eco-efficiency means reducing energy/resource consumption and environmental impacts mainly by *technical or design changes* to products, systems or manufacturing processes, as opposed to reducing environmental impacts through changes in human behaviour or consumption patterns.

In this and the next section, I consider whether the eco-efficiency reductions in environmental impacts achievable through green design, ecodesign and sustainable design are sufficient to tackle environmental problems such as climate change or whether more radical sustainable innovation approaches are needed. The *Consumption* block then argues that even sustainable innovation may not be sufficient and that changes in consumption and lifestyle are also required.

> The T307 DVD shows how sustainability strategy and environmental legislation have influenced product development at Royal Philips Electronics. You'll see that Philips practises all four strategic approaches to designing for the environment. View 'Philips: design for sustainability' either at a convenient time during this section or after reading the Philips case study in Section 9.

I'll now look in more detail at the green design and ecodesign approaches.

7.2   Green design

As noted above, green design is the development of products with a reduced impact on the natural environment. An influential report, *Green Products by Design*, from the US Office of Technology Assessment, defined green design as:

> ... a design process in which environmental attributes are treated as *design objectives*, rather than as *constraints*...green design incorporates environmental objectives with minimum loss to product performance, useful life or functionality.

(Office of Technology Assessment, 2005, p. 7)

However, green design is limited by focusing on tackling one or two environmental objectives associated with the production, use or disposal of a product.

Case study   The Remarkable pencil

A good example of green design conceived primarily to meet a single environmental objective – materials conservation – is the Remarkable pencil produced from plastic vending cups, 3.5 million of which are collected for recycling each week in the UK. Each pencil uses one recycled (hard or expanded) polystyrene vending cup encasing a core of recycled polystyrene mixed with graphite. Developing this product involved innovation in the process for manufacturing pencils as well as product design and innovation.

The Remarkable Company produces a range of stationery products made from recycled materials, including rulers made from recycled polystyrene packaging; notepads from recycled paper and board; pencil cases and mouse mats from recycled tyres; and pens from recycled computer printers. The range also includes colouring pencils made from Forest Stewardship Council (FSC) certified timber. As you can see from Figure 40, product and graphic design plays an important role in development of these greener products to make them attractive to different buyers.

(a)

(b)

Figure 40 Green design. (a and b) Stationery products, including notebooks and pencils, made from recycled materials. Lava Sky is one of a range of different designs aimed at different markets. Source: Remarkable Ltd

Other examples of green design, primarily designed for one environmental objective, are a stool made from forest thinnings (Figure 41a), a waste paper basket made from recycled newspaper; a coffee filter with a reusable metal mesh rather than a disposable paper filter, or a waterless urinal that uses a filter instead of flushing. These all help to reduce the consumption of virgin materials or water. Other examples of green design include condensing gas central heating boilers (Figure 41b) or folding bicycles to reduce reliance on the private car, which both help to reduce fossil fuel consumption and associated emissions. A third group of green products include a detergent that avoids use of certain water-polluting chemicals, or socks made from naturally brown- or green-coloured, organically grown cotton, so reducing the use of pesticides and eliminating dyes in production (Figure 41c).

Figure 41   More examples of green design. (a) Materials focus: stool made by Trannon from forest thinnings that would normally be wasted. (b) Energy focus: condensing gas central heating boiler averages over 90% energy efficiency compared to 55 – 65% for an older conventional boiler. (c) Toxic emissions focus: Foxfibre socks made from naturally brown- or green-coloured, organically grown cotton, therefore reducing pesticide use and eliminating chemical dyes. Sources: (a) Trannon; (b) Baxi Potterton; (c) Datchefski, 2001, p. 86

Often, green design focuses on a single environmental objective perceived by consumers, politicians or pressure groups as important, such as recycling materials or preserving wildlife, even if these are, arguably, not the most urgent priorities. A focus on such objectives is often formalised in legislation, such as the EU Packaging and Packaging Waste Directive. Hence, there is considerable work on the design of packaging to reduce the amounts of waste going to landfill and to promote recycling (Figure 42a). The design and innovation involved varies from the relatively straightforward, such as Philips replacing the plastic inner packaging for its shavers by moulded cardboard, to the extensive R&D involved in developing the Q-CELL air-filled packaging (Figure 42b).

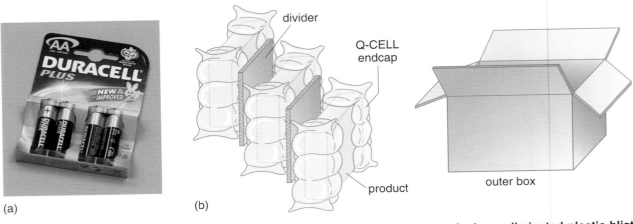

(a)

(b)

Figure 42   Green packaging designs. (a) Materials focus – Duracell battery packs have eliminated plastic blister packaging and enabled batteries to be packaged in a single recyclable material, cardboard. (b) Materials, energy and waste focus – Q-CELL packaging employs interlinked air-filled plastic pockets to absorb impacts. This patented design uses less material and is far lighter than plastic foam packaging for items ranging from electronic equipment to books, therefore saving materials and energy for transport. After use, Q-CELL can be deflated and returned to the supplier for reuse or recycling. Sources: (a) http://www.informationinspiration.org.uk; (b) Kirby and Gabbitas, 1996, pp. 92–96

Environmental regulation, legislation and agreements have encouraged the design of greener products that tackle other specific environmental issues, such as eliminating certain materials or chemicals, controlling the discharge of toxic wastes, or specifying energy efficiency. As noted above, EC restriction of hazardous substances (RoHS) legislation bans the use of toxic metals in the manufacture of electrical and electronic products.

International agreements to phase out ozone-depleting CFCs, and to tackle climate change by reducing emissions of greenhouse gases, have meant that European refrigerator manufacturers had eliminated CFCs and their alternatives from their products by the late 1990s. Instead, manufacturers adopted the technology pioneered in the Greenfreeze refrigerator that uses a hydrocarbon-mix refrigerant and insulation blown by also using hydrocarbons. At the same time, EU legislation on energy labelling has encouraged manufacturers to improve the energy efficiency of refrigerators.

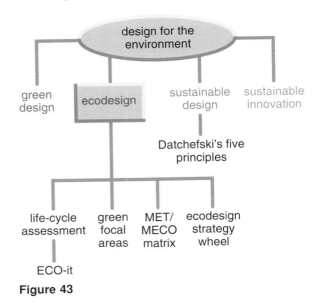

Figure 43

7.3   Ecodesign

Because green design focuses on one or two particular environmental objectives, it has limitations. This is because it may not address the most significant impacts of a product, or at least only some of them.

7.3.1 Materials, energy and toxicity

As there are so many environmental issues, there are many ways a designer or product development team could design or redesign a product to be greener. However, if you examined a large number of greener products, you would find that most are designed with a primary focus on one of three broad environmental objectives:

- materials – reducing material or resource consumption

- energy – reducing fossil-fuel energy consumption

- toxicity – reducing polluting emissions or toxic wastes.

In Table 2, I've listed some examples of products that employ different design approaches to address each of these three environmental objectives.

Table 2   Designing for the environment based on a focus on different environmental objectives

Environmental objective[1]	Design approach	
Materials (reducing material or resource consumption)	use less materials or water	**examples:** rechargeable batteries; water saving dishwashers and washing machines; concentrated detergents in refillable packs; waterless urinals and composting toilets
	made from recycled or waste materials or components	**examples:** road surfacing material made from used car tyres; packaging made from recycled plastics; garden furniture made from recycled plastic waste; jewellery made from recycled electrical components
	made from renewable materials and sustainable sources	**examples:** furniture made from forestry wastes; timber from sustainably managed forests
	designed for durability, repair and maintenance	**examples:** long-life automobiles; high-quality classic clothing designs

Environmental objective[1]	Design approach	
	designed for reuse, upgrading, remanufacture or recycling	**examples:** computers designed for upgrading; laser printer toner cartridges remanufactured from used cartridges; TV receivers redesigned for disassembly, materials recycling and component recovery
Energy (reducing fossil-fuel energy consumption)	energy efficiency	**examples:** energy-efficient domestic appliances; compact fluorescent lamps; condensing boilers; hybrid petrol–electric cars
	energy conservation	**examples:** heat-reflecting window glass; thermostatic radiator valves
	renewable energy source	**examples:** solar water heaters; wind-up radio or torch; bicycles; photovoltaic roof tiles
Toxicity (reducing toxic pollution and damage to ecosystems)	reduced use of toxic, hazardous or ecologically damaging chemicals/ materials	**examples:** aerosols that operate on compressed gas rather than hazardous liquid propellants; organic solvent-free gloss paints; HCFC-free refrigerators; phosphate-free detergents
	pollution control equipment	**examples:** cyclonic diesel engine exhaust cleaning system; vehicle catalytic converters

[1] Some products may match more than one objective

It is unlikely that any greener product could fully meet all the environmental requirements at once. But in moving beyond single-issue green design to a more systematic ecodesign approach, a designer or design team would apply their technical knowledge and creativity in an attempt to address as many of the materials, energy and toxicity issues as possible.

For example, a designer might try to reduce fossil fuel energy consumption by designing for energy efficiency, or to use a renewable energy source. Likewise, reducing resource consumption could involve designing to use less water or materials, recycled materials or renewable materials, or designing for disassembly and recycling at the end of the product's life. And design to reduce toxic emissions and waste requires design to avoid use of hazardous or ecologically damaging chemicals or materials.

7.3.2 Life-cycle-based ecodesign

I've said that one approach to ecodesign is for the designer to try to address as many of the materials, energy and toxicity objectives as possible. Several ecodesign checklists exist to aid this approach (examples of such ecodesign checklists are given later in this section). However, this approach is not always enough to provide the best ecodesign solution. It is often necessary to *assess* and *balance* the environmental impacts over the product's physical life cycle. The life cycle from raw materials extraction, through manufacture and use, to final disposal is often referred to as from 'cradle to grave'.

For example, compact fluorescent lamps (CFLs), which you met in the *Invention and innovation* block, help both to save fuel through their greater energy efficiency and conserve materials through their longer life. However, even these ecological products may reduce the impact in one phase of their life cycle at the expense of increased environmental impacts in another phase. Compact fluorescent lamps contain small amounts of mercury, a toxic pollutant, and so their adoption raises the issue of controlling mercury releases during manufacture and safe disposal of the lamps. However, burning coal to generate electricity also releases mercury and so, depending on how the electricity to power the lamp is produced, over their total life cycle CFLs may either increase or reduce mercury emissions compared to conventional incandescent lamps (EPA, 2002). The need to assess and balance all the different environmental impacts of a product throughout its life means that there is a need for a life-cycle approach to designing for the environment.

To address this issue, an approach to design for the environment emerged in the 1990s, known as life-cycle design (LCD). Life-cycle-based ecodesign is a relatively new approach to product development, but one that is gaining increased use in multinational companies including Philips (as you can see on the T307 DVD), Electrolux, AT&T and Dow Chemical.

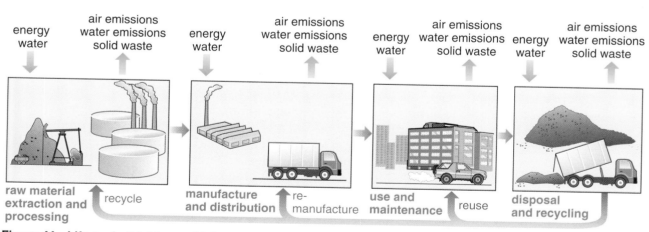

Figure 44   Life-cycle thinking and LCA Source: based on OTA, 2005
This shows the main stages in the physical life cycle of a product and the inputs and outputs to the environment at each stage, and the possible reuse, remanufacturing or recycling of materials

Life-cycle thinking

The first step in a life-cycle ecodesign approach is to *think* in terms of a product's physical life cycle when designing. That means considering the environmental impacts that may arise at every phase of the product's life: from the extraction of the raw materials used in its manufacture, to what happens to the product at the end of its life (Figure 44). Then, having identified possible impacts, attempt to minimise them. Many designers and companies do not go beyond life-cycle thinking when designing for the environment.

Case study Blue Line furniture

Blue Line is a small British office furniture manufacturer that attempts to minimise its products' environmental impacts throughout their life cycle.

- *Raw materials.* All products manufactured by the company since the year 2000 use 30%–100% timber by volume from sustainably managed forests certified by the Forest Stewardship Council (FSC), with the rest comprising recycled timber (Figure 45). The company also works with environmental organisations and universities to develop alternatives for non-timber components. For example, it hopes to replace a number of plastic items with recycled 'bio-plastic'.

- *Transport.* To reduce transport fuel consumption, wherever possible the company uses local suppliers. For example, instead of sourcing metalwork from overseas, it only uses local manufacturers and engages them in minimising the environmental impact of their operations.

- *Manufacture.* Offcuts of timber are not sent to landfill but given, free of charge, to partner organisations. The company participates in a project aimed at recycling sawdust into compost.

- *Distribution.* No packaging is used to deliver Blue Line products: they are blanket-wrapped and delivered by trained installation crews.

- *Reuse.* The company has a 'buy-back' policy for customers purchasing new products. These products are refurbished and sold through an active second-user market.

Sources: http://www.informationinspiration.org.uk/
http://www.blueline.uk.com, (accessed 8.2.05)

(a)

(b)

Figure 45 (a) Blue Line desk designed using life-cycle thinking and made using FSC certified timber. (b) Forest Stewardship Council label.
Source: (a) Blue Line

life-cycle assessment

a technique for quantifying the impacts of a product over its physical life stages from 'cradle to grave'

Life-cycle assessment

After life-cycle thinking, the next step is to try to assess the impacts using a technique known as life-cycle assessment (LCA). LCA attempts to *quantify* all the environmental impacts of a product throughout its life cycle, starting from the impacts arising from extracting and processing the raw materials involved in its manufacture, through impacts from its manufacture, distribution and use, to those associated with its reuse, refurbishment, recycling or end-of-life disposal (see Figure 44).

The purpose of LCA is to identify at which phases of the life cycle the greatest impacts occur, in order to help decide the best strategy for reducing and balancing them. LCA therefore helps avoid focusing on minor environmental impacts while ignoring the major ones. LCA also aims to help avoid making a change in a product that reduces one environmental impact, but at the expense of increased impacts elsewhere. For example, the use of recycled materials may reduce a product's durability and hence require its more frequent replacement, or a more durable moving component may be heavier and therefore make the product less energy efficient. These negative effects may be hidden or ignored and may outweigh any environmental improvements.

A simple example of the use of LCA should make this clearer.

Case study Axis jug kettle

The small appliance industry is fiercely competitive and manufacturers are always on the lookout for ways to gain an advantage. An Australian company, MEC-Kambrook, worked with an EcoReDesign team at the Royal Melbourne Institute of Technology to develop an eco kettle that would appeal to environmentally conscious consumers. The resultant Kambrook Axis kettle was launched in Australia in 1996.

An earlier attempt by another company, GBK, to produce a greener kettle for the US market had focused on the single issue of designing a kettle for disassembly and recycling at the end of its life. However, a life-cycle assessment carried out on an existing Kambrook kettle showed clearly that the overwhelming environmental impacts of a kettle are the greenhouse gas emissions and solid wastes (ash and other solids) from the coal-fired power stations generating the electrical *energy* consumed during its *use*. Solid waste from discarded kettles was a relatively minor impact (Figure 46). The team therefore decided to concentrate its main design effort on reducing the kettle's energy consumption.

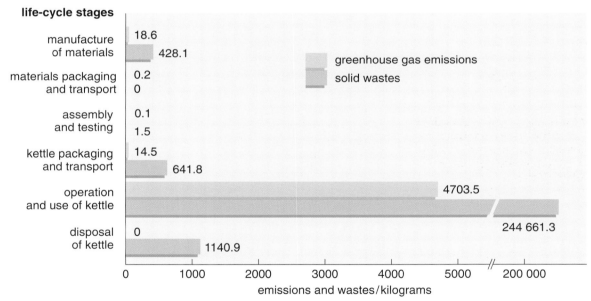

Figure 46   Life-cycle impacts of a kettle, focusing on greenhouse gas emissions and solid wastes
Source: Sweatman and Gertsakis, 1996, p. 97

Without major technical innovation, there was little scope for improving the efficiency of the electrical heating system, so the team focused on how people used kettles to see if this provided ideas for saving energy (a user-centred approach, as discussed in the *Markets* block). Studies of users showed that few people used a water gauge to judge how much to fill the kettle; and they often reboiled the kettle even when the water was hot enough to make a drink.

MEC-Kambrook's design brief to the product development team (as well as the usual requirements of safety, attractive styling and ease of use) included environmental objectives – reducing energy consumption, providing the user with information on water temperature, and designing for fewer materials, disassembly and recycling. The team was larger than usual for a small appliance development project; it involved 16 people: designers and engineers, physicists, social researchers, an environmental consultant and a polymer specialist, and had support from Australian government funding.

The EcoReDesign team came up with three energy-saving improvements to existing jug kettles: improve the water gauge by placing it at the top of the kettle; keep the water hot by giving the kettle an insulating double-wall with an air gap; and include a temperature-sensitive coloured patch to show if the kettle needs reheating. Tests showed that the kettle required 6% less energy to boil and 25% less energy if reheated up to 45 minutes later, representing an overall energy saving of up to one-quarter (25%) over previous designs if the temperature gauge was used to avoid unnecessary reboiling. Figure 47 shows some preliminary sketches and the final design of the Axis kettle.

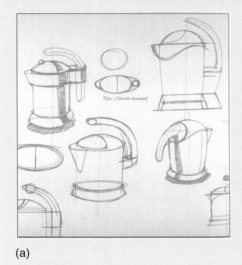

(a)

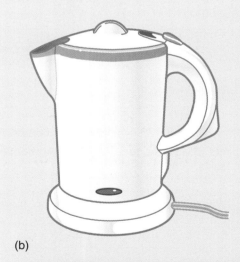

(b)

Figure 47 MEC–Kambrook Axis jug kettle: (a) preliminary sketches; (b) drawing of the final design Sources: (a) Sweatman and Gertsakis, 1996, p. 98; (b) Gertsakis, Lewis and Ryan, 1997, p. 80

In addition, the team made several environmental improvements in choice of materials and manufacturing methods. The kettle's weight was reduced by 16%, the proportion by weight of recyclable polymer was nearly doubled, and the number of different materials and components nearly halved. Snap fits and ultrasonic welding of plastic parts replaced glues and screws and those parts have internationally recognised code marks to facilitate disassembly and recycling.

Sources: Gertsakis, Lewis and Ryan, 1997, pp. 80–81; Sweatman and Gertsakis, 1996

Can you think of another design idea to reduce the energy consumption of a kettle based on the EcoReDesign team's user research?

A kettle with a reservoir that dispenses the correct amount of water needed for one or more cups of drink onto the heating element. An eco-kettle with this feature was launched in 2005.

Full LCA-based ecodesign: BeoVision LX5500 TV

As the Kambrook kettle example shows, ecodesign, even if based on a relatively simple LCA, may involve a larger product development team plus extra cost and design effort. Not surprisingly, ecodesign based on a full quantitative LCA can be a complex and expensive process. To give you an idea of what is involved, an example is LCA-based ecodesign of a Bang & Olufsen TV set conducted as part of a Danish government/industry/university programme called Environmental Design of Industrial Products. Table 3 shows part of the LCA inventory of the numerous resources and environmental impacts involved in the production of materials, manufacturing, use and disposal of the Beovision LX5500 70 cm colour TV, including transport at the different phases. The TV weighs 43 kg, power consumption is 100 W and 3 W in standby mode.

Look carefully at Table 3 overleaf. Identify the most significant resources consumed and environmental impacts over the TV's physical life cycle. These major LCA inventory items should then suggest ideas for the ecodesign of a new, greener TV. *Hint*: these are the larger quantities or more toxic emissions.

Table 3 shows that coal and other fuels used to generate electricity to operate the TV during the *use* phase of the life cycle (including standby power) account for 99% of all the energy resources consumed and for over 80% of all the CO_2 emissions. Energy for TV use also produces most of the air pollutants, including sulfur dioxide, nitrogen oxide and heavy metal particles, and 70% of the waste.

Most of the remaining energy and associated emissions are for the production of materials and for manufacturing. Other significant resources and impacts include the 1.7 kg of toxic lead oxides used to make the TV's picture tube and the lead and carbon monoxide emissions from international transport of materials and components and distribution of the final product.

Table 3 Resource consumption, emissions and waste over the life cycle of the Beovision TV

		Units	Production of materials	Product manufacturing	Use	Disposal	Transport	Total
Resource consumption								
crude oil		g	**15 100**	2300	**59 700**	10	3300	80 000
natural gas		g	**59 800**	6200	**43 000**	6	200	109 000
coal		g	4500	14 300	**215 000**	200	16	234 000
brown coal		g	1030	610	**160 000**	–	–	162 000
uranium ore		g	0.05	0.06	22	–	–	22
water for hydropower		litre	3900	870	**88 000**	9	~0	92 800
aluminium	Al	g	710	23	11	~0	~0	700
iron	Fe	g	3200	–200	4	~0	~0	3000
copper	Cu	g	800	0	0	0	0	800
manganese	Mn	g	23	–1	–	–	–	22
nickel	Ni	g	5	–	–	–	–	5
zinc	Zn	g	46	–	–	–	–	46
barium carbonate	$BaCO_3$	g	3100	–	–	–	–	3100
lead oxide	Pb_3O_4	g	**1700**	–	–	–	–	1700
calcium carbonate	$CaCO_3$	g	1950	–160	7	~0	~0	1800
quartz	SiO_2	g	15 400	–290	–	–	–	15 000
sodium carbonate	Na_2CO_3	g	3800	0	0	0	0	3800
sodium chloride	NaCl	g	615	12	18	~0	~0	650
soft wood		g	530	80	**10 200**	1	~0	10 800
groundwater		litre	–	44	–	3	~0	47
surface water		litre	~0	1	~0	~0	~0	1
unspecified water		litre	180	280	33	~0	1	500
Materials and ancillary substances for which resource consumption is not included								
paint		g	–	319	–	–	–	319
various materials*		g	–	2160	–	–	–	2160
various ancillary substances*		ml		6000	–	–	–	6000
Emissions to air								
carbon dioxide	CO_2	g	**166 000**	62 000	**1 051 000**	13 000	6400	1 300 000
carbon monoxide	CO	g	200	22	680	43	750	1700
nitrogen oxides	NO_x	g	**1000**	210	**4200**	17	170	5600
sulfur dioxide	SO_2	g	550	260	**9300**	3	18	10 100
dinitrogen oxide	N_2O	g	18.1	5.2	84.8	~0	0.2	108

	Units	Production of materials	Product manufacturing	Use	Disposal	Transport	Total
unspecified particulates (dust)	g	76	87	500	~0	5	670
hydrocarbons HC	g	470	350	5050	4	9	5900
volatile organic compounds VOC	g	1.6	38	1.1	~0	0.4	41
unspecified aldehydes	g	~0	0.16	3.75	~0	~0	3.9
2-propanol, isopropanol	g	–	1.8	–	–	–	1.8
benzene	g	0.032	–	–	–	–	0.032
butyl acetate	g	–	10	–	–	–	10
butyl diglycolacetate	g	–	15	–	–	–	15
ethyl acetate	g	–	88	–	–	–	88
phenol	g	–	0.25	–	–	–	0.25
toluene	g	–	4	–	–	–	4
trichlorethylene	g	–	1.1	–	–	–	1.1
unspecified xylene	g	–	51	–	–	–	51
dioxin	mg	–	1 E-06	–	128 E-06	~0	130 E-06
epichloryhdrin	mg	37	–	–	–	–	37
arsenic AS	mg	~0	1	99	~0	~0	100
lead Pb	mg	**990**	1	140	~0	**1330**	1460
cadmium Cd	mg	~0	~0	12	~0	~0	12
copper Cu	mg	1	4	99	140	~0	240
mercury Hg	mg	~0	1	18	~0	~0	19
manganese Mn	mg	410	260	–	–	–	670
vanadium V	mg	28	39	2770	~0	~0	2800
Emissions to water							
chemical oxygen demand COD	g	18	~0	1	~0	~0	19
total nitrogen tot-N	g	1	8	2	~0	–	11
total phosphorus tot-p	g	–	0.15	–	–	–	0.15
hydrocarbons HC	g	6.7	0.06	1.4	~0	0.06	8.2
unspecified oil	g	5.9	0.3	2.4	~0	~0	8.6
phenol	g	0.04	~0	0.035	~0	~0	0.08
arsenic As	mg	15	–	–	–	–	15
lead Pb	mg	2	–	–	–	–	2
cadmium Cd	mg	8	–	–	–	–	8
chromium (VI) Cr	mg	–	9	–	–	–	9
copper CU	mg	55	3	–	–	–	58
mercury Hg	mg	0.003	0.033	–	–	–	0.036

		Units	Production of materials	Product manufacturing	Use	Disposal	Transport	Total
manganese	Mn	mg	–	0.2	–	–	–	0.2
nickel	Ni	mg	52	28	–	–	–	80
zinc	Zn	mg	48	35	–	–	–	83
Waste								
unspecified hazardous waste		g	0.03	0.001	–	–	–	0.03
unspecified dust containing heavy metals		g	–	2	–	–	–	2
unspecified industrial waste		g	64	1	–	–	–	65
unspecified radioactive waste		g	0.004	0.01	3	–	–	3
unspecified slag and ashes		g	330	1220	**41 000**	8200	8	50 800
unspecified bulk waste		g	5600	**33 600**	**125 000**	**30 000**	9	194 000

Notes to Table 3:
– means that no information is available for the life-cycle stage in question
~0 means that the figure is small compared to the other stages of the life cycle
* only amounts above 100g included; B&O has made an inventory of the consumption of a large number of materials and ancillary substances; for reasons of transparency, these have here been collected under the entries 'various materials' and 'various ancillary substances'.
The product manufacturing stage includes both the production at B&O and at the subcontractors. The stated figure for resource consumption and emissions is therefore from all the manufacturers.
(Source: extracts from Wenzel et al 1997, pp. 381–382)

This detailed LCA showed the dominance of the use phase of the life cycle in the TV's environmental impacts, followed by materials production and manufacture. This suggests possible ideas for the ecodesign of a new TV.

- Replace the conventional CRT tube with a more energy-efficient liquid crystal display.

- Reduce the operational and 10% standby energy consumption of the TV by using circuits and components that use less power.

- Combine the TV with a video or DVD recorder to reduce standby power consumption and the materials and components required.

- Incorporate a device to switch off the TV when not being viewed.

- Make the casing from an alternative to painted plastic to reduce materials energy and resource consumption and facilitate recycling.

It could be argued that given the dominance of the use phase for almost all energy-consuming products – from TVs to cars – a full LCA isn't needed to decide how to make environmental improvements. However, for more detailed ecodesign decisions such as the selection of materials for a TV, a focused LCA study can be useful, as the following case study shows.

Case study | Materials for the Beovision Avant casing

Bang & Olufsen carried out another LCA study in order to help its product development team choose the environmentally least-damaging materials for the main casing of a combined TV and video system, the Beovision Avant (Figure 48). Other requirements for the casing were low cost, few components, rapid assembly and minimum changes from existing designs.

Figure 48 Beovision Avant combined 28-inch TV and hi-fi video recorder with active loudspeakers and motorised stand, 1995. TV-DVD models were introduced in 2001 Source: Bang & Olufsen

Three materials were assessed in the LCA: moulded polystyrene; fibreboard (woodchips bound with glue), these first two assumed to be incinerated at the end of life; and aluminium veneered with wood, with the metal recycled at the end of life.

Figure 49 gives the results of the LCA. The data are quite complicated to interpret and you don't need to understand the details. But essentially the assessment shows that over its life cycle the plastics casing produces the highest impacts. These are measured in terms of: (a) *global warming*; (b) *acidification* of the air, rain and soil (which damages forests, fish and buildings); (c) nutrient enrichment from excess nitrogen or phosphorus (which damages fragile water and land ecosystems); and (d) effects on *human health* through exposure to toxic chemicals.

The veneered aluminium casing, even if recycled, has the highest impacts in terms of *wastes* – including nuclear and bulk waste, slag and ash – mainly due to the large amount of electricity used in its production.

The wood fibreboard casing has the lowest impacts in almost every category. Bang & Olufsen therefore chose fibreboard as the most environmentally-friendly material for the casing for the Avant. Fibreboard's main drawback is that the formaldehyde used in its production can cause harmful emissions affecting workers in the factory and, some argue, also in the home.

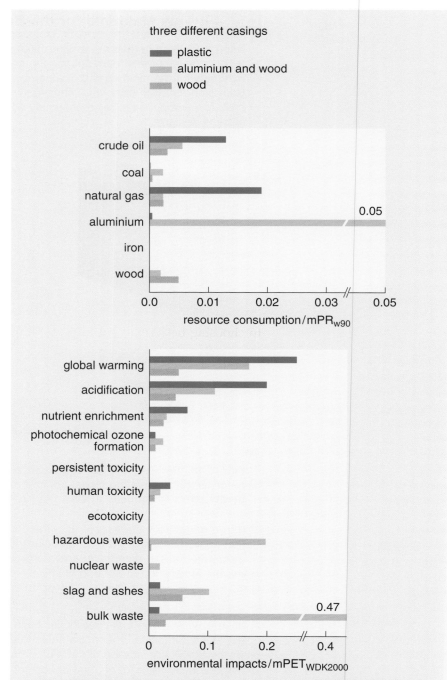

Figure 49 Total environmental impacts over their life cycle of three materials for the main casing of the Beovision Avant combined TV–video system Source: Wenzel et al, 1997, pp. 123, 410
The unusual unit mPR_{w90} stands for milli-person reserves (world 1990). This is a measure of resource depletion due to production of the product, where 1 mPR_{w90} is one-thousandth of the average global reserves for a particular non-renewable resource available per person in 1990. The unit $mPET_{WDK2000}$ stands for one-thousandth-person equivalent weighted environmental impacts relative to target emissions for either the world (W) or Denmark (DK) in 2000.

By better electronics design, the product development team also managed to reduce the power consumption of the Avant by about 7%, leading to reduced environmental impacts in use.

Source: Wenzel et al, 1997, pp. 409–411

In the above example of the casing for the Avant TV-video system, the LCA produced a clear-cut result – wood was the most environmentally friendly material. However, LCAs often do not produce clear results. Another LCA of the same product, material or component may produce different results depending on its measures and assumptions.

Moreover, it can be difficult to choose which is the most important of the various environmental impacts identified or to compare and trade off one type of impact with another. For example, if the choice had been only between the plastic and aluminium casing for the Avant, then the decision would have been much more difficult. The LCA impacts would depend on whether it was assumed that the material was reused, recycled or discarded at the end of life.

In choosing between environmental impacts, product developers would have had to decide whether a casing that produced less global warming and acid rain over its life cycle (aluminium) was preferable to one that generated less waste (plastic). They would also have to decide whether conserving aluminium resources was more important than conserving the oil and gas needed to make plastic. And, of course, this narrowly defined LCA does not address the total environmental impacts of this large, feature-laden TV-video unit, most of which would arise during its use.

LCA therefore often can only inform subjective judgements rather than make objective decisions for ecodesign.

7.4 Ecodesign tools

As you've seen, a full LCA is complex, time-consuming and expensive. In addition, LCA can only provide information to guide design decisions. In practice, therefore, the majority of ecodesigns are based on less-detailed, more-qualitative assessments of likely impacts of a product over its life cycle. In this section, therefore, I'll introduce some simplified tools for ecodesign. You'll be given exercises in applying them to identify how to reduce product environmental impacts.

I'll also introduce some life-cycle assessment software, called ECO-it, which should enable you to conduct a simplified quantitative LCA of a product or component at the detail design stage.

7.4.1 Green focal areas

The simplest ecodesign tool is a checklist to remind the designer or design team to try to achieve important environmental objectives during product development.

For example, Royal Philips Electronics has developed an ecodesign checklist that requires its design teams to address five so-called green focal areas during the product creation process:

1   reduction in *weight*

2   reduction or elimination of *hazardous substances*

3   minimising *energy consumption*

4   increased *recycling* and reduced *disposal*

5   reduction, reuse and recycling of *packaging*.

Philips adopted this simplified approach after trying to introduce more complex LCA-based methods for ecodesign. The green focal areas have proved to be a practical way for Philips' product developers to address the business's ecodesign priorities aided, if required, by simplified life-cycle assessment software.

If you've viewed the video 'Philips: design for sustainability' on the T307 DVD, you'll have heard about the green focal areas. You'll find more about ecodesign at Philips in a detailed case study in Section 9.

7.4.2 MET matrix

I noted earlier in this section that attempts to lessen the environmental impacts of products generally fall into three categories:

● Reducing material/resource consumption.

● Reducing fossil fuel energy consumption.

● Reducing toxic emissions/wastes.

Notice that Philips' five green focal areas address these objectives; but materials/resource consumption is covered by three of the focal areas on the T307 DVD (1, 4 and 5).

You also saw that the main phases in the physical life cycle of a product are:

● raw materials extraction and processing

● manufacture

● transport and distribution (materials, components, finished product)

● use and maintenance

● end-of-life reuse, remanufacture, recycling or disposal.

A useful qualitative LCA method that combines these categories and phases is the so-called MET matrix, where: M = materials; E = energy and T = toxic emissions or waste (Table 4). The matrix acts rather like a checklist to ensure that a design team identifies and considers all the important areas of impact throughout the life cycle of the product.

Table 4   MET matrix for qualitative life-cycle assessment

Environmental impact areas	Life-cycle phase*			
	Materials supply and manufacture	Transport and distribution	Use and maintenance	End of life
Materials				
Energy				
Toxic emissions and waste				

* Some life-cycle phases are combined in this MET matrix to make it less cumbersome

To conduct the assessment, you should do the following. For a given product, such as a particular model of washing machine, at each life-cycle stage (manufacture, distribution, and so on) you note important environmental issues or impacts for each of the areas of materials use, energy consumption and toxic emissions or waste. In this way, you attempt to identify any important environmental problems for as many cells of the matrix as possible.

In the 'Materials' row you should pay particular attention to inputs of materials – for instance copper – that are non-renewable and/or a depleting resource and/or create significant emissions during manufacture. You should also note if materials, products or components are discarded, rather than reused, remanufactured or recycled.

In the 'Energy' row, particularly note emissions of carbon dioxide, sulfur dioxide and nitrogen oxides due to high fossil fuel or electricity consumption during manufacture, distribution and use of the product. Note also inputs of materials that involve a large amount of energy in processing – aluminium is one example.

In the 'Toxic emissions and waste' row, note any outputs to air, water or land at any stage of the life cycle that are harmful to human health, wildlife or the ecosystem.

To identify the impacts, it is of course necessary to have some information about the product, such as what it is made from, the approximate weights of materials in it, and substances consumed during use.

> The CES Selector database on the T211 DVD provides useful information on the 'Eco properties' and 'Impacts on the environment' of many materials (when MaterialUniverse is set to Edu Level 2).

Information on energy label ratings, energy consumption, and where relevant water consumption for products is often available from the manufacturer, or found in internet databases and consumer reports such as those in *Which?* magazine.

Given sufficient knowledge and information, you or the design team may be able to rank the impacts identified in the matrix according to their relative importance, for example on a qualitative scale where:

$\triangledown$ $\triangledown$ $\triangledown$ = serious negative impact(s)
$\triangledown$ $\triangledown$ = significant negative impact(s)
$\triangledown$ = minor negative impact(s)
$\triangle$ = no apparent impact(s) or positive impact(s)

This process can be repeated for another product – for example the most energy-efficient available washing machine – because it is sometimes easier to *compare* products relative to each other using such qualitative judgements. For example, on the Materials row under the 'Materials supply or manufacture' phase, a particular washing machine might be noted to have relatively low environmental impacts because of its all-steel construction, while another machine might have higher impacts because it uses reinforced plastics for parts such as the outer tub.

At the 'Use' life-cycle phase, the first washing machine might be noted to have relatively high 'Energy' consumption because it is rated 'C' on the energy label, compared to the 'A+' energy rating of the most energy-efficient machine. Likewise, at the 'Use' phase under 'Materials', the first washing machine might be noted to have relatively high detergent consumption compared to the most efficient machine. This high detergent consumption also will pose issues concerning water pollution under the 'Toxic emissions/waste' element of the 'Use' phase.

Under Materials at the 'End-of-life' phase of the life cycle, the machine that uses reinforced plastic components would pose more problems for recycling than the all-steel machine. But this is likely to be a relatively minor issue compared to that of energy, detergent and water consumption in use.

Clearly, there is much judgement and estimation involved in such an assessment. Nevertheless, a qualitative LCA provides a clearer picture of environmental impacts than guesswork and can be helpful to identify areas where improvements to the design, technology or use of the product can reduce environmental impacts. For example, an obvious improvement to the less-efficient washing machine would be to reduce its energy, water and detergent consumption levels to those of the most efficient.

Case study Veromatic coffee machine

Table 5 shows an MET matrix completed for a professional coffee machine made by a Dutch company, Veromatic (Figure 50a). The items in bold are those that the ecodesign team consider serious ($\triangledown\triangledown\triangledown$) or significant ($\triangledown\triangledown$), and so need most urgent attention. These include inefficient energy use by the boiler, the lack of recovery of potentially valuable components, and the possibility of toxic pollution from landfill disposal of the machine's printed circuit board.

(a)   (b)

Figure 50 **(a) Drawing of Veromatic Cafeja coffee machine for professional use. (b) New model Veromatic Ultima drinks dispensing machine.** Sources: (a) Based on Brezet and van Hemel, 1997, p. 72; (b) Veromatic International BV

Table 5 **MET matrix applied to the Veromatic Cafeja professional coffee machine**

Life-cycle phase	Environmental impact area		
	Materials (input-output)	Energy (input-output)	Toxic emissions (output)
Production and supply of materials and components	copper (exhaustible material); zinc (exhaustible material)	high energy content of materials	fire retardants in printed circuit boards; flow improvers for injection moulding; polystyrene: benzene emissions; polyurethane: isocyanate emissions due to painting and gluing
In-house production	metal waste; plastic waste	process; energy	
Distribution			
Utilisation operation	plastic cups (1472 kg PS)*; filter paper (90 kg)*; used coffee (2944 kg)*; plastic spoons (110 kg PP)*; cleaning materials; polluted water (4160 l)*; water filters (20)*	▽▽▽**inefficient energy use by boiler**; transport energy	

Life-cycle phase		Environmental impact area		
		Materials (input-output)	Energy (input-output)	Toxic emissions (output)
	servicing	easily broken parts	transport of service providers	
End-of-life system	recovery	▽▽ **no reuse of valuable parts such as boiler; disposal of coffee machine (37 kg); no recycling of plastics; packaging; plastics (5 kg); print plates (0.5 kg)**		
	disposal			▽▽ **printed circuit boards (0.5 kg); copper; zinc**

▽▽(▽)**Items requiring attention**
*Figures are calculated for a consumption of four cups of coffee daily by 40 persons, during 10 years.
Source: Adapted from Brezet and von Hemel et al, 1997, p. 73

After the team had identified key areas for improvement, they generated ideas for reducing environmental impacts. For example, the team produced the following ideas to improve the energy efficiency of the machine's boiler:

● Insulate the boiler casing.

● Install a time switch to turn off the boiler after a given time.

● Use a smaller boiler.

● Use the minimum temperature required to make good coffee.

Subsequently, the team used a more systematic technique for generating environmental improvement ideas, which I'll outline below in Section 7.4.

On the T211 DVD, there is an interactive exercise using an MET matrix to compare the original Freeplay clockwork radio (described in a case study in Section 9) and small battery-powered radios, and then identify areas for environmental improvement. You may wish to attempt this exercise now or at the end of the section.

7.4.3 MECO matrix

A similar qualitative LCA method to the MET matrix is the MECO matrix, where M = materials, E = energy, C = chemicals, O = other. ('Other' could refer to noise, product life, and so on.). As for the MET, you draw up a matrix of the environmental impact areas against life-cycle stages (see Table 6) to identify impacts and areas for improvement.

Table 6   MECO matrix for qualitative life-cycle assessment

Environmental impact areas	Life-cycle phase*			
	Raw materials	Manufacture	Use and maintenance	End of life
Materials				
Energy				
Chemicals				
Other				

* Transport and distribution may also be included for all phases

BeoVision LX5500 TV (continued)

I described ecodesign of the BeoVision LX5500 television based on a detailed LCA earlier in a case study. Its designers also carried out a much simpler MECO matrix assessment. The following matrix cells suggested several areas of significant impact and ideas for environmental improvement (Wenzel et al, 1997, pp. 135, 400).

- 'Materials/Raw materials' and 'Materials/End of life' cells suggested using wood instead of plastic for the casing, and recycling the TV's copper and aluminium content.

- 'Energy/Use and Maintenance' cell suggested reducing power consumption by improved electronics.

- 'Chemicals/Manufacture' cell suggested not painting the casing.

- 'Others/Use and Maintenance' cell suggests increasing the product's lifespan from 10 to 15 years.

7.4.4 ECO-it life-cycle assessment software

The MET and MECO matrices provide a qualitative indication of the most likely priority areas for environmental impact and improvement. However, you can try to be more precise by using some software, called ECO-it, provided on the T211 DVD. ECO-it enables you to calculate the quantitative life cycle environmental impacts of a product or component with results presented as a composite number called Eco-indicator points (Pt) or one-thousandth points (mPt). 1 Pt represents the annual environmental damage produced by the activities of 1000 average Europeans calculated from a weighted combination of three elements:

- *Human health.* The severity of diseases, and years lost through premature death from environmental causes due to climate change, ozone layer depletion, carcinogenic (cancer-causing) effects, respiratory effects and nuclear radiation.

- *Ecosystem quality.* The effect on species diversity from eco-toxicity, acidification, eutrophication and land-use.

- *Resources.* The surplus energy needed in future to extract lower-quality mineral and fossil resources.

ECO-it provides an LCA of a domestic coffee maker, 'Coffee-It', that has similar components to the Veromatic professional coffee machine in the above case study.

Exercise 5   ECO-it – coffee-maker evaluation

If you haven't done so, install ECO-it from the T211 DVD. Start it and attempt the following exercises, referring as needed to the instructions provided separately.

1   Using ECO-it's demonstration mode, show that the main impacts of the Coffee-it coffee maker example occur in the Use phase of its life cycle.

2   Identify any other areas where worthwhile ecodesign improvements to the coffee maker might be made.

3   Explore the effects on Eco-indicator points of making changes to the coffee maker's materials, production process and/or energy source for brewing coffee.

4   Compare the ECO-it results for the Coffee-it with improvements suggested by the MET matrix for the Veromatic coffee maker.

7.4.5 Ecodesign strategy wheel

The MET and MECO matrices and ECO-it are useful for identifying important areas of environmental impact over the life cycle and for generating some initial ideas for reducing those impacts.

To help generate environmental improvements more systematically, another qualitative technique, the ecodesign strategy wheel, is very useful.

> I'll apply the ecodesign strategy wheel in some practical exercises below; you should also find it useful in your project.

Eight ecodesign strategies

The ecodesign strategy wheel provides eight broad approaches or ecodesign strategies for improving the environmental performance of a product throughout its life cycle (Figure 51).

The eight strategies are:

1   *Selection of low-impact materials*. For example, recycled materials or materials that do not involve too much energy or pollution for extraction and processing.

2   *Reduction of materials usage*. For example, reduction in weight and/or volume of materials used.

3   *Optimisation of production techniques*. For example, a production process that uses less energy and/or produces less pollution and waste.

4   *Optimisation of distribution system*. For example, less and/or reusable packaging, and/or a more energy-efficient method of transport and/or of organising distribution.

5   *Reduction of impact during use*. For example, lower energy consumption in use, or fewer consumables required during use, or less waste arising from use.

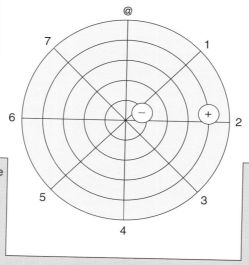

product system level

7 optimisation of end-of-life system
reuse of product
remanufacturing/refurbishing
recycling of materials
safer incineration

6 optimisation of initial lifetime
reliability and durability
easier maintenance and repair
modular product structure
classic design
strong product-user relation

@ new concept development*
dematerialisation
shared use of the product
integration of functions
functional optimisation of product
(components)

product component level

1 selection of low-impact materials
cleaner materials
renewable materials
lower energy content materials
recycled materials
recyclable materials

2 reduction of materials usage
reduction in weight
reduction in volume transported

5 reduction of impact during use
lower energy consumption
cleaner energy source
fewer consumables needed
cleaner consumables
no waste of energy or
consumables

3 optimisation of production techniques
alternative production techniques
fewer production steps
lower or cleaner energy
consumption
less production waste
fewer or cleaner production
consumables

product structure level

4 optimisation of distribution system
less, cleaner or reusable packaging
energy-efficient transport mode
energy-efficient logistics

*New concept development has been given the symbol @ because it is more innovative than the other seven strategies

Figure 51 Ecodesign strategy wheel. Moving round from the 1 o'clock position are seven strategies for designing or redesigning a product to reduce environmental impacts at different phases of its life cycle plus one strategy for providing the product's function with a new concept. Source: Brezet and van Hemel, 1997, pp. 81, 346

6   *Optimisation of initial lifetime.* For example, a more reliable or durable product, or a product that is easy to maintain and repair, or a classic design that doesn't go out of fashion.

7   *Optimisation of end-of-life system.* For example, reusing the product, or refurbishing the product, or recycling its materials, or safe disposal.

8   *@ new concept development.* This strategy is different and more radical than the other seven. It involves considering whether the product's essential functions might be performed by some alternative system that produces fewer environmental impacts. Could the product be integrated with other products and so save resources? Could the product be replaced by a dematerialised service, for example email replacing conventional mail? (This email example gave rise to the @ symbol for this strategy.) Could the product be shared by more people or organisations, like a hired tool or a car-sharing scheme?

Ecodesign strategy number eight combines the sustainable design and sustainable innovation approaches introduced earlier, and which I'll discuss further in Section 9.

If desired, you can plot the environmental profile of the original product and of the improved product after the implementation of the relevant ecodesign strategies on the central wheel.

Ecodesign guidelines and rules of thumb

For each of the strategies, there are guidelines and 'rules of thumb' to aid designers. These are provided in a United Nations Environment Programme (UNEP) Manual on *Ecodesign* (Brezet and van Hemel, 1997, pp. 144–158).

For example, for ecodesign strategy 5: Reduction of impact during use, option 'Fewer consumables needed', the manual provides the following guideline:

> The aim of this principle is to design the product so that fewer consumables are needed for its product functioning ...

plus these 'rules of thumb' to help achieve the guideline:

> design the product to minimise the use of auxiliary materials, e.g. use a permanent filter in coffee makers instead of paper filters, use the optimal shape of filter to ensure optimal use of coffee
>
> minimise leaks from machines that use high volumes of consumables
>
> study the feasibility of reusing consumables – reusing water in the case of a dishwasher.

> (Brezet and van Hemel, 1997, p. 153)

Ecodesign rules of thumb

A full list of the UNEP *Ecodesign* manual's guidelines and rules of thumb is several pages long, so I've provided separately an edited list that is most likely to be of value to you in your project work. You can also find this and other ecodesign checklists on the internet.

Case study Veromatic coffee machine (continued)

The MET matrix provided some initial ideas for environmental improvement of the Veromatic coffee machine. The ecodesign strategy wheel offers a more systematic method of generating ecodesign improvement ideas.

For example, below are some ecodesign ideas generated by considering each of the eight strategies in turn, aided by the guidelines and rules of thumb provided separately.

1   Selection of low-impact materials.

Find alternatives for non-ferrous metals that involve high environmental impacts during their production. (It may be possible to substitute some copper or zinc parts, or use recycled metals.) Use the same, or mutually compatible, materials for different parts (to facilitate recycling).

2   Reduction of materials usage

Reduce the size of the machine – for example by placing parts closer to each other, expressing quality through good design rather than large size. Combine different functions in one part – for example use one container instead of three for the coffee-making ingredients.

3 Optimisation of production techniques

Consider the production methods to see if there are any ways of reducing impacts arising from manufacture of the machine. For example, design the product to avoid production processes that create harmful emissions and waste; recycle wastes; or use renewable energy sources for manufacture.

4 Optimisation of distribution system

Reduce the amount of packaging materials – for example protect only the corners of the machine with packaging.

Make the packaging returnable for reuse, made from recycled materials and/or recyclable.

Use local suppliers for materials and components.

Minimise distribution by modes of transport with a high environmental impact – for example road and air.

5 Reduction of impact during use

Insulate the boiler casing.

Install a time switch to turn off the boiler after a given time.

Using the minimum temperature required to make good coffee.

Design the product to use minimum consumables – for example replace paper with permanent filters; disposable with reusable cups.

(Most of these options were also generated by considering the MET matrix for the coffee machine.)

6 Optimisation of initial lifetime

Use materials and finishes that do not deteriorate or wear quickly.

Make product easy to maintain and repair – for example indicate which components need regular servicing; how the product can be opened to insert replaceable components.

Design the machine so that it does not quickly look dated.

7 Optimisation of end-of-life system

Design the machine for easy disassembly – for example by using snap rather than screwed or glued joints.

Use recyclable materials – for example avoid reinforced plastics.

Reuse parts that are still economically valuable.

8 @ new concept development

Lease or rent the machine so that all machines are returned to the manufacturer for refurbishment, remanufacture or recycling. Under EC WEEE legislation return to the manufacturer or an agent for recycling is required.

Integrate some functions. For example, design a multifunctional coffee machine, so it can dispense tea and hot water as well as coffee, so avoiding the need for several devices.

Improvement ideas from using the eight ecodesign strategies, such as the ideas listed above, should at this stage normally be generated without considering their feasibility, market or environmental benefits, so as not to inhibit consideration of all possible options. To narrow down the ideas, it is necessary to evaluate them by considering their technical and financial feasibility, the constraints and opportunities of the market, and their environmental benefits. This will inevitably throw up issues that require further research and investigation before an improvement can be taken further, or eliminated.

For example, evaluation by the ecodesign team of the ideas for improving the coffee machine, against criteria of feasibility, market and likely environmental benefit, eliminated many of the options on practical grounds, such as changes to the existing packaging. But the evaluation indicated further investigation of the feasibility of insulating and reducing the size of the boiler, and of reusing certain parts.

The result of these feasibility studies produced a short-term and a longer-term strategy for the ecodesign improvement of the coffee machine. The short-term strategy involved reducing the boiler size from 4 to 2 litres and insulating it with polystyrene foam, which was estimated to reduce energy loss to air from 44% to 7%. The longer-term strategy involved setting up a return and recovery system for old coffee machines, and redesigning the machine to reuse certain valuable components, recycle other components and materials, and only shred parts that could not be reused or recycled.

(Adapted from Brezet and van Hemel, 1997, pp. 83–87)

The T211 DVD includes an interactive exercise to learn a technique, called Selection Matrix, for evaluating design ideas against a set of criteria. You may wish to view this at some point and consider its relevance to your project.

Let's see now if you can apply the ecodesign strategy wheel to another task.

Exercise 6   Ecodesign strategies – mobile phone

The mobile phone manufacturer Nokia has given you the task of redesigning one of their phones to minimise its environmental impacts. A life-cycle assessment has identified production of the electronic components as the primary source of environmental impacts and the energy consumed in use by the phone and its charger as secondary. The main materials used in manufacture of the phone are plastics (32% by weight, mainly ABS and polycarbonate), copper (19%), and aluminium (9%). (Data from Nokia, 2003, 2005.)

Look at the ecodesign strategy wheel and using the eight strategies listed, and referring as necessary to the ecodesign rules of thumb (provided separately), suggest at least five ideas for ecodesign improvement options.

You may find it helpful to use the worksheet on ecodesign improvement options (Table 7) to enter your ideas. The CES Selector database on the T211 DVD and Nokia's and other mobile phone manufacturers' internet sites should also provide useful information and ideas. Spend 15–20 minutes on the task before looking at the discussion below.

Table 7   **Ecodesign strategies worksheet**

Strategy	Improvement options
1 selection of low-impact materials	(a) (b) (c)
2 reduction of materials usage	(a) (b) (c)
3 optimisation of production techniques	(a) (b) (c)
4 optimisation of distribution system	(a) (b) (c)
5 reduction of impact during use	(a) (b) (c)
6 optimisation of initial lifetime	(a) (b) (c)
7 optimisation of end of life system	(a) (b) (c)
8 @ new concept development	(a) (b) (c)

Source: Brezet and van Hemel, 1997, p. 344

Discussion

Table 8 shows some ideas for ecodesign improvement options to reduce the environmental impacts of a Nokia mobile phone.

Table 8   **Ecodesign improvements for a mobile phone**

Strategy	Improvement options
1 selection of low-impact materials	(a) use recycled plastics for internal parts of casing, and advise suppliers to use recycled copper in electronic components (b) ensure materials banned under RoHS legislation, e.g. cadmium, mercury, are not used; avoid other hazardous materials, e.g. PVC for electrical insulation (c) minimise use of aluminium, as the phone is a short-life product
2 reduction of materials usage	(a) further reduce size of phone to minimise materials consumed (b) design a small, simple to use phone with basic functions
3 optimisation of production techniques	(No ideas for this strategy)

Strategy	Improvement options
4 optimisation of distribution system	(a) minimise packaging (b) use recycled materials for packaging
5 reduction of impact during use	(a) provide a solar or human-powered charger for batteries (b) design a charger that automatically switches off or signals when the phone is charged (c) design a phone with integral hands-free kit to minimise users' exposure to microwave radiation
6 optimisation of initial lifetime	(a) provide downloadable software from the internet to upgrade phone functions (b) interchangeable covers or casings to extend life (c) create a classic-looking, repairable and upgradeable design that will not date too fast
7 optimisation of end of life system	(a) supply an envelope to return phone for reuse, refurbishment or recycling at the end of its life (b) use 'smart materials' to disassemble the phone into sections when heated (Nokia has developed a prototype, Figure 52a)
8 @ new concept development	(a) design a combined main house cordless and mobile phone (as introduced by BT in 2005) (b) design a human-powered phone (the o2 UK network for sustainable design has created a concept model, Figure 52b)

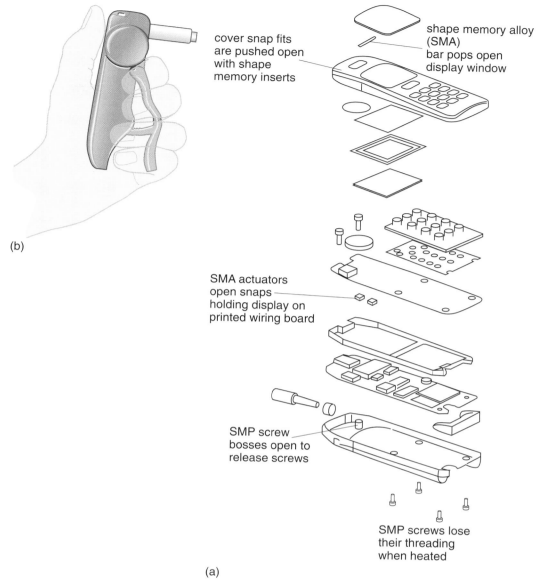

cover snap fits
are pushed open
with shape
memory inserts

shape memory alloy
(SMA)
bar pops open
display window

SMA actuators
open snaps
holding display on
printed wiring board

SMP screw
bosses open to
release screws

SMP screws lose
their threading
when heated

(b)

(a)

Figure 52 Novel ideas for ecodesign improvements of mobile phones. (a) Nokia prototype mobile phone, with shape memory alloy (SMA) actuators and shape memory polymer (SMP) screws that actively disassemble the phone into sections when heated. (b) Concept for a human-powered mobile phone comprising a hand-powered generator plus phone module. One minute of squeezing the Japanese Nisso AlladinPower device provides power for just one minute of talk time. Source: (a) adapted from www.nokia.com

You could repeat the above exercise for a product of your own choice – for example, one made or used by an organisation where you work, or the product idea in your project.

7.5 Socio-economic influences on ecodesign

So far, I've discussed products, such as mobile phones, kettles or TV sets, for which ecodesign is uncontroversial, but that may only produce relatively minor reductions in the total environmental impacts of production and consumption. Improving such products, although useful, is not going to solve global environmental problems. But what about products that have major environmental impacts? In 2005, UK transport, mainly private cars, accounted for 30% of total carbon emissions, as well as a high proportion of air pollutants. Domestic heating, lighting and appliances accounted for another 28% of UK carbon emissions (HM Treasury, 2005). Ecodesigning vehicles, heating systems, lights and appliances (especially refrigerators, freezers and washing machines) could therefore make a real difference.

However, you've seen that the environmental issue(s) addressed when designing for the environment often depend on legislation and the views and priorities of business, consumers, politicians and pressure groups. A good example is the design of greener cars. This has been influenced as much by social, economic and political factors as by 'scientific' LCA studies and life-cycle ecodesign.

Figure 53 shows some of the environmental impacts of a conventional motor car throughout its life cycle. The main materials used in the manufacture of cars are steel, aluminium, copper, plastics and glass. Extracting and processing these materials involves the consumption of large amounts of energy and water, the production of various emissions to air and water and the creation of large amounts of solid waste. During manufacture and assembly of the car, further energy, water, paints and other inputs are required, producing more emissions and solid waste.

After sale and during its useful life, the car will consume large amounts of petrol or diesel fuel, producing emissions of CO_2, carbon monoxide (CO), unburned hydrocarbons and nitrogen oxides that are harmful to human health and/or the environment. During its life, a car will also require the replacement and disposal of many parts and components, including tyres, battery and exhaust pipe. At the end of its life, the car will normally be broken up and many of its materials and components recycled, involving further energy consumption and emissions. Finally, materials, such as toughened and laminated glass, rubber and fabrics, which cannot easily be recycled, are buried as solid waste.

LCA studies have shown that at least 80% of the environmental impacts of cars occur during the *use* phase of their life cycle, mainly because of the fossil fuel they consume and the resultant exhaust emissions (Mildenberger and Khare, 2000, p. 208). Therefore, ecodesign of cars should focus on the 'Reduction of impact during use' strategy. This would include measures to reduce fuel consumption, for example by fuel-efficient engine design, improved aerodynamics, lightweight construction (Figure 54a), and innovations such as hybrid petrol–electric cars and electric cars powered by hydrogen fuel cells (Figure 54b).

In the USA, federal government CAFE (Corporate Average Fuel Economy) regulations forced car manufacturers to produce improvements in fuel consumption from the late 1970s, but since the enormous growth in US sales of 4-wheel drive sport utility vehicles (SUVs), which until 2008 to 2010 are exempt from the regulations, average fuel consumption has worsened again. Likewise, although many European and Japanese manufacturers have developed more fuel-efficient cars, market and commercial demands for increasing

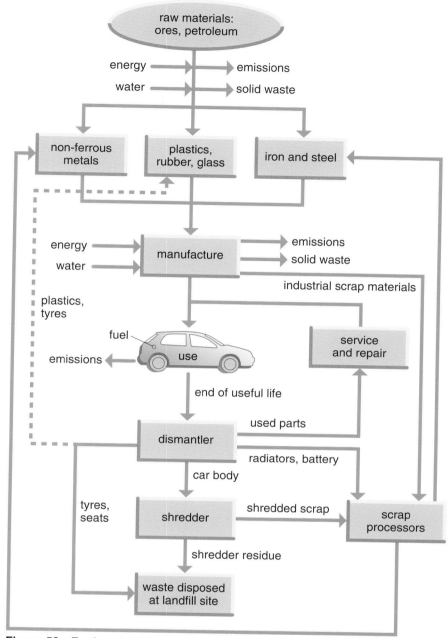

Figure 53 Environmental impacts of a motor car throughout its life cycle
Source: adapted from Thurston, 1994, p.31

performance, size, and crashworthiness, and features such as air conditioning, have cancelled out the efficiency gains (Figure 55).

Most European car manufacturers and legislators have until recently tried to avoid US-style legislation on fuel economy by concentrating on single-issue green design approaches or less environmentally worthwhile ecodesign strategies, especially 'Optimisation of production techniques' and 'Optimisation of the end of life system'. For example, many manufacturers introduced water-based paints to reduce emissions of volatile organic compounds (VOCs) during car production. The EU End-of-Life Vehicles Directive, outlined earlier, focuses on the end-of-life phase by requiring manufacturers to design cars that facilitate dismantling, reuse and recovery. EU regulation from

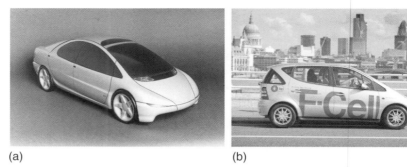

(a)   (b)

Figure 54   (a) E-Auto prototype lightweight aluminium car designed for a fuel economy of about 140 mpg, but not put into production. (b) Daimler–Chrysler Necar F-cell hydrogen fuel-cell car. The F-cell is based on the Daimler Chrysler NECAR prototypes and a Mercedes A-class vehicle and was in limited production. Sources: (a) Cranfield University in Open University 2003, p. 117; (b) Mercedes Benz UK

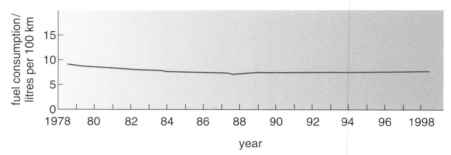

Figure 55   Average fuel consumption of EU petrol cars, 1978–1999. Note: CO_2 emissions are closely linked to fuel consumption. Source: Open University, 2003, p. 39

the early 1990s affecting 'Reduction of impact during use' did not focus on fuel economy but on reducing car exhaust pollutants such as carbon monoxide, hydrocarbons and nitrogen oxides by requiring cars to be fitted with catalytic converters and getting oil companies to improve fuel quality. Indeed, catalytic converters increase rather than improve fuel consumption.

However, since 1999, European regulations turned to the issue of fuel economy. Regulations require display of a label on all new cars in showrooms, listing their CO_2 emissions and fuel consumption. In addition, the UK levies road tax on cars in bands according to their CO_2 emissions. From 2005, the UK introduced a voluntary scheme, in anticipation of future EU legislation, which provides labels on cars rated for their CO_2 emissions per km and colour-coded from A to F, similar to the successful EU energy label on refrigerators and other appliances. (Figure 56). All UK car brands signed up to this labelling scheme and European manufacturers also volunteered to reduce CO_2 emissions per km of new cars sold in the EU by a readily achievable target of 25% by 2012 (Open University, 2003).

Figure 56 Car fuel economy label (based on the EU energy label shown in Figure 62) Source: Department for Transport

The effect of these regulations and agreements is uncertain, but as noted above, so far most fuel economy improvements have been cancelled out by consumers continuing to trade up to larger, more powerful cars, and driving further and faster. Given this, the extent to which eco-efficiency, such as ecodesign improvements in car fuel economy, can solve global environmental problems is explored in the *Consumption* block.

Case study | Volvo cars

Volvo is one manufacturer that has attempted to use a type of LCA in designing and marketing its vehicles. Volvo publishes an environmental product information (EPI) statement that provides consumers with comparative information on the way each of its car models affects the environment throughout its life cycle. It is therefore possible to select the least environmentally harmful model of Volvo according to its impacts relative to other Volvo cars, in the production, use and end-of-life phases. For example, the life-cycle diagram for the 2005 Volvo S40 1.6 shows that in use its CO_2 emissions are about midway between the best and worse Volvo model and that its emissions of controlled pollutants are over 80% better than a standard European car.

But this provides little information on the relative importance of the different impacts or how Volvo cars compare with those of rival brands. So, Volvo's LCA doesn't help people select the greenest car on the market, which would give Volvo's designers stronger incentives to make major ecodesign improvements. However, the fuel economy label (Figure 56) does provide comparative information on CO_2 emissions of all car models and should help provide such incentives.

Key points of Section 7

- Four strategic approaches to designing for the environment are: (i) green design, (ii) ecodesign, (iii) sustainable design and (iv) sustainable innovation. The first three are eco-efficiency approaches for reducing environmental impacts by means of increasingly radical technical or design changes. Sustainable innovation goes beyond technical solutions to include socio-technical changes to product–service mixes or systems.

- Green design is limited to tackling one or two environmental objectives. Ecodesign attempts to tackle as many of the materials, energy and toxicity impacts of a product as possible.

- Life cycle based ecodesign attempts a balanced reduction in environmental impacts throughout a product's life cycle – from raw materials extraction to end of life.

- There are many ecodesign methods and tools, ranging from full quantitative LCA studies, through qualitative matrix methods to simple checklists. Full LCAs are very complex and can only guide design decisions, so ecodesign is usually based on simpler methods and tools.

- The eight ecodesign strategies provided by the ecodesign strategy wheel is one of the most effective methods for generating environmental product improvement ideas.

- Ecodesign improvements to products such as kettles and TVs, which have relatively minor effects on the total environmental problem, are generally uncontroversial. However, attempts to reduce the impacts of socially and economically important products, such as cars, is influenced by socio-economic and political factors which may hamper the use of life cycle ecodesign approaches.

8 Ecodesign processes and organisation

In Part 1 of this block, I introduced several models that describe the process and organisation of new product development (NPD). In this section, I'll discuss how those models apply to designing for the environment.

8.1 Integrating ecodesign into NPD

Essentially, there is no difference between an NPD project that attempts to reduce the environmental impacts of a new product and one that does not. In a green or ecodesign project, environmental objectives are simply another factor that the designer or design team considers along with the usual design factors of performance, cost, appearance, ergonomics, safety, ease of manufacture, and so on.

For example, the ISO 14000 series of international environmental management standards includes ISO 14062 (2002) for 'integrating environmental aspects into product design and development', which sets out a design process model similar to those in Figures 9a to 9c in Section 2 (Greenwood, 2004, p. 44). Likewise, Electrolux's integrated product development process, shown as Figure 29b in Section 4, provides for all design factors, including environmental ones, to be considered during NPD and then signed off at key checkpoints, as in the stage-gate model discussed in Section 2. The main difference, of course, is that in a green or ecodesign project one or more individuals or departments have to provide the necessary knowledge and expertise to integrate environmental factors into the NPD process.

From an organisational viewpoint, therefore, designing for the environment adds yet another area of expertise to be co-ordinated. This means that green/ecodesign projects have to be undertaken either by a dedicated team, or via a matrix structure, such as described in Section 3. It's important that environmental objectives are considered from the beginning of NPD. Environmental objectives, such as minimising energy consumption in use, should therefore be included as criteria in the product design specification and the design checked against these criteria as it is developed.

Before all this can happen, the business concerned has to be committed to designing for the environment by having an environmental strategy or policy and being capable of implementing that policy in NPD projects. This often means having an environmental 'champion' or department to change staff attitudes towards environmental issues and to promote green/ecodesign strategies and methods in the business. It may require training designers and others in ecodesign tools such as those outlined in the previous section. And, as you will see in the case studies of Hoover and Philips in this and the next section, changing attitudes, developing an environmental policy, and integrating ecodesign into NPD is an organisational learning process that takes time.

Case study Bang & Olufsen

In Section 7, you learned about the use of LCA and other ecodesign tools at Bang & Olufsen, the upmarket Danish audiovisual manufacturer, for the development of a Beovision TV and a TV-video system. At Bang & Olufsen, environmental considerations are integrated into normal product development routines from the beginning and treated in the same way as other considerations such as component purchasing, manufacturing and after-sales service (Wenzel et al, 1997, p. 408). A dedicated project team undertakes NPD, with help from environmental and other specialists as required.

Figure 57 shows Bang & Olufsen's NPD process and how LCA and other ecodesign tools fit in. As you can see, it is similar to the design process models introduced in Section 2, but with the addition of a simplified LCA at the planning and specification stages (idea to goal definition in Figure 57) to help set the environmental objectives by reference to an existing ecodesigned product. The new product is then developed through concept and detailed design and manufacturing stages (concept to production). During these stages, several ecodesign tools are applied, including design for recycling (to ensure maximum recycling at end of life); LCA, such as carried out for the Beovision Avant (to help choose energy-efficient and low-polluting materials and production processes); and cleaner technology (to consider new environmentally preferable manufacturing technologies).

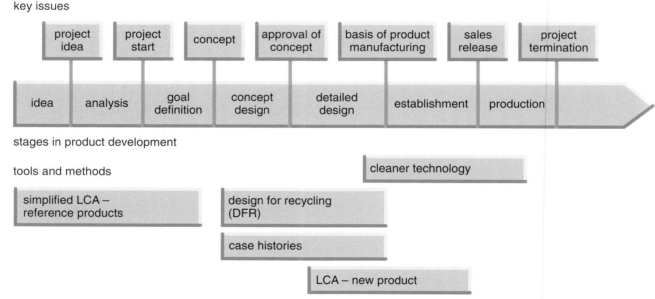

Figure 57 **Bang & Olufsen's product development process showing the integration of LCA methods and ecodesign tools** Source: Wenzel et al, 1997, p. 408

8.2 Learning ecodesign at Hoover

I want now to focus on a product development project that involved a company shifting its approach from green design towards ecodesign as the organisation gradually learned about designing for the environment. At the same time, the company moved from a mainly linear to a more concurrent, team-based NPD process. This learning took place as its senior management drew up an environmental policy and participated in a major LCA study of washing machines for the launch of the EU ecolabel. However, as you'll see, there's much more the company could do to reduce environmental impacts by applying the eight ecodesign strategies that I introduced in Section 7.

At the end of the case study, which is several pages long, there is an exercise for you to do, so you may wish to look at this first.

Case study   Hoover washing machines

Hoover, one of the world's best-known domestic appliance brands, has made washing machines in Britain since 1948. This case study, covering a period from 1990 to 2005, discusses the creation of Hoover's original New Wave range of greener washing machines, first launched in 1993 after a four-year development programme and £15 million investment in new manufacturing plant (Roy, 1997, 1999). The New Wave washing machines were the first products awarded an EU ecolabel for exceeding set criteria for energy, water and detergent consumption and wash performance. The case study then discusses the replacement of New Wave by new ranges from 1998 onwards, after sale of the Hoover European Appliance Group to the Italian white goods manufacturer, Candy. Finally, I apply the ecodesign strategy wheel to identify possible additional measures Hoover could take to further reduce the environmental impacts of its products.

Product planning

The New Wave project originated in the late 1980s when Hoover's washing machines were losing market share.

The company had already decided to buy in pre-coated steel for its washing machine cabinets, and as a result remove the labour-intensive and dirty process of welding and spray-painting sheet steel. Developments in materials meant that the outer tub could now be moulded from reinforced plastics, rather than fabricated from steel. There was therefore an opportunity to develop a new product range to accompany the new manufacturing processes.

Hoover also recognised that a growing number of consumers were demanding 'greener' products, and that its competitors had already taken a lead in this market. Zanussi, for example, in 1986 launched its 'Jetsystem' range in which the water is pumped to the top of the machine and sprayed down on the clothes instead of wetting them in the drum, therefore saving water and energy. Hoover was aware too of EU plans to label washing machines for their environmental performance.

Environmental performance was of course only one aspect of the planned new machine's appeal. Hoover wished to move upmarket from its previous position in the washing machine market.

NPD process

Although development of the New Wave involved serious consideration of environmental factors for the first time, no changes to Hoover's already highly systematic stage-gate type NPD process were required. The environment just added another factor to be considered together with all the usual product development issues, and so the design team 'learned as it went along'. The main change was in the organisation of NPD: from the former linear process to a more concurrent process with a closely knit, cross-functional project team.

Specification

At the start of the New Wave project, senior managers from Engineering, Marketing, Manufacturing and Finance met to agree the business and market specification for the new range. This formed the basis of the technical specification. Environmental impacts were a key factor in the specification. Hoover recognised – before this had been shown by formal LCA studies – that any reduction in the environmental impacts of the new machine would depend mainly on minimising water and energy consumption in use.

The next step was to convert the technical specification into feasible concept designs. This involved three parallel tasks:

● Researching how to reduce water, energy and detergent consumption.

● Deciding how the machine was to be engineered and manufactured. The team eventually decided to fix together the pre-coated steel panels for the cabinet by using mechanical joints instead of traditional welding. Rough concept sketches for a machine with a pre-coated steel cabinet and a plastic outer tub were produced by the design team (Figure 58a).

● Design of the visual and ergonomic aspects of the machine. Hoover's industrial designers intended that the machine's appearance would enable it to stand out from competing products and produced a number of concept sketches of the machine (Figure 58b).

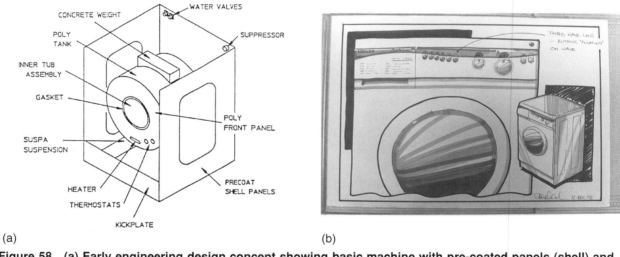

(a) (b)

Figure 58 (a) Early engineering design concept showing basic machine with pre-coated panels (shell) and plastic outer tub (tank). (b) Early design sketch showing wave shape applied to control panel. Source: Hoover European Appliance Group

Concept design

In order to reduce the amount of energy, water and detergent consumed by the machine, Hoover's R&D group carried out a feasibility study of several new concepts, including 'spray paddles' – perforated agitator paddles in the drum to scoop up water from the base of the drum and shower it over the clothes (Figure 59a). This concept would avoid infringing the patents on pumped systems used by other manufacturers (Figure 59b).

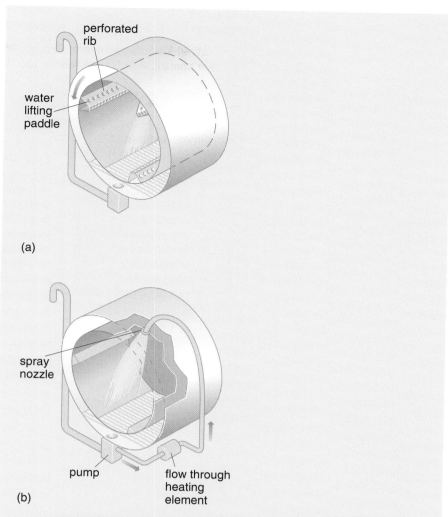

Figure 59   Diagrammatic comparison of: (a) passive spray paddle system similar to that used on Hoover washing machines; (b) pumped spray system similar to that used on Zanussi Jetsystem machines
Source: Open University, 1999b, p. 33

The new wash process required development of an electronic control system to allow more precise control of the wash cycle than was possible with an electromechanical timer. In addition, the decision to use a plastic outer tub allowed a sump to be moulded in, therefore allowing the drum and tub to fit more closely than previously and the machine to operate with less water.

Design and development

The research concepts had then to be developed into a practical design. This involved Hoover product engineers developing and testing mock-ups and prototypes to get a consistently good wash performance. In parallel, component designs were finalised for manufacture. By substituting snap-fits for screws and other fixings, and the single-piece moulded tub, the new machine had one-third fewer parts than the previous range.

Environmental policy and ecolabelling

The original impetus for the environmental aspects of the New Wave project was the growing market for greener washing machines. However, soon after the project had begun, Hoover senior managers began to consider what the company should do to respond to environmental issues more generally. This resulted in the board issuing an environmental mission statement in 1990. This committed the company to a life-cycle approach to design, stating that the company aimed: 'To adopt the best practical environmental methods in the design, production, packaging, use and disposal of its products, whilst continuing to improve their benefits to the consumer' (Hoover, 1990).

Also in 1990, the European Union announced its ecolabelling scheme. Hoover was one of four manufacturers to participate in developing ecolabelling criteria and specifications for washing machines. The ecolabelling scheme is based on a life-cycle approach and, in 1991, a life-cycle assessment (LCA) was commissioned to establish criteria for the washing machine ecolabel. The study showed that over 95% of the environmental impacts of washing machines occur during their use (Figure 60).

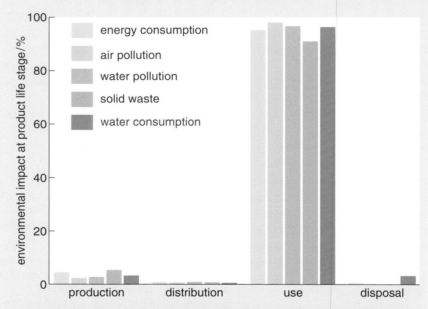

Figure 60 Life-cycle assessment of washing machines, showing the percentage contribution to total environmental impacts at the product life stages from cradle to grave Source: Open University, 1999b, after PA Consulting Group, 1991, p. 37

The LCA for the ecolabel confirmed Hoover's focus on reducing the water, energy and detergent consumption of New Wave, but also indicated other areas of environmental impact that may have had to be considered before the launch of the range, if it was to meet the ecolabel criteria. The director of engineering development, who was responsible both for Hoover's environmental policy and developing the New Wave, acted as 'environmental champion' to ensure these issues were addressed. Without this senior management commitment, it is unlikely that the project would have moved towards the use of a full life-cycle approach to ecodesign.

SECTION 8

Ecodesign

Hoover therefore began to consider the environmental impacts arising from production, distribution and disposal as well as the use of the New Wave. However, this was well into the NPD process, rather than from the beginning as recommended for ecodesign projects.

Production

Use of pre-coated steel for the cabinet gave Hoover energy savings from welding and drying, and eliminated toxic emissions of volatile organic compounds (VOCs) from spray-painting. But the company was careful not to claim environmental improvements until the emissions from the supplier of the pre-coated steel had been evaluated. Fortunately for Hoover, this retrospective assessment showed that a real overall environmental benefit had been achieved.

Distribution

Hoover examined the advantages and disadvantages of a cardboard pack versus a polystyrene pack shrink-wrapped with polythene. Both cost similar amounts and could be recycled, but the company concluded that polystyrene performed better and had the edge on environmental grounds, being lighter to transport and using less water and energy to manufacture.

To reduce transport costs and fuel consumption, Hoover commissioned a new design of trailer for transporting its washing machines. This enabled more machines to be carried in each load, and significantly reduced the number of vehicle movements required for distribution.

Disposal

A reduction in the number of fixings in the machine – adopted mainly for production reasons – made the New Wave easier to take apart for recycling. Recycling would also be facilitated by reducing the variety of plastics used and identifying them by type.

Marketing the New Wave

The New Wave range was first launched, and its EU ecolabel awarded, in 1993. By 1997, the Hoover New Wave and its successor range were still the only appliances to have been awarded the voluntary ecolabel (Figure 61). Other washing machine manufacturers did not apply for an ecolabel because they did not consider the marketing advantage was worth the ecolabel fees. Another factor was the introduction of compulsory EU energy labelling in 1996. The energy label for washing machines (Figure 62) gives a ranking for energy efficiency, wash and spin performance plus information on water consumption and noise, and so rewards manufacturers of the most efficient machines, unlike the simple pass-fail criterion of the ecolabel.

133

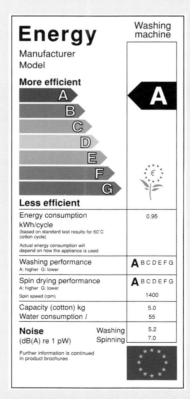

Figure 61 Part of a 1996 Hoover brochure, showing the top-of-the-range, 1500-rpm spin speed, New Wave Plus 5. This range gained an EU ecolabel (shown above), plus a B rating for energy efficiency on the energy label. Source: Hoover European Appliance Group

Figure 62 EU energy label for washing machines, which rates energy efficiency plus washing and spinning performance on a scale from A to G
Source: europa.eu.int

Nevertheless, Hoover believes that the ecolabel was an important factor in selling the New Wave, especially in the environmentally aware German and Danish markets. Environmental factors are generally less important in the UK market where price and performance are crucial, and so the New Wave was first promoted mainly on its money-saving aspects. However, in later sales material, environmental friendliness and the ecolabel were strongly featured, targeting environmentally conscious consumers.

The investment in the development and manufacture of the New Wave was also employed to produce washing machines aimed at price-sensitive volume UK and Southern European markets. By substituting electromechanical for electronic controls, Hoover developed lower-priced ranges that saved energy, water and detergent compared to previous models, but did not quite satisfy the ecolabel criteria.

Beyond New Wave

In May 1995, the Hoover European Appliance Group was sold by its US owners to the Italian Candy Group. After a transition period, in 1997–98 the company's new owners introduced significant changes in both the design of Hoover's washing machines, and in the processes used to manufacture them.

These changes were the result of joint development work by Candy and Hoover engineers and designers, which brought the laundry products and production processes at Hoover into line with those in other parts of the Candy Group.

Production

The main change was a reintroduction of production plant to make washing machine cabinets from painted and welded steel, replacing the pre-coated steel plus mechanical fastening process installed for the New Wave ranges. New plant, costing £17m and involving a production system similar to that used prior to the New Wave project – but using more modern equipment – was reintroduced for several reasons. First, to be compatible with other parts of the Candy Group, thereby giving flexibility to switch production between factories. Secondly, given advances in production technology such as the use of powder coating and automated welding, it was more economic.

Product design

Four new washing machine designs were launched in 1998 to replace the New Wave and associated ranges. Although the New Wave range had helped Hoover break into environmentally sensitive export markets, sales were not as great as had been expected, at least in the price-sensitive UK market. In addition, there was growing price competition plus demand for further reductions in energy and water consumption since the introduction of energy labelling.

As well as a need to reduce production costs and improve reliability, the new designs were driven by the desire to obtain better ratings on the energy label than achieved by the New Wave models. In the new top-of-the-range model, this was achieved by several changes to the wash process developed from concepts used on other Candy machines. These included a pumped water recirculation system, in which water from the sump is sprayed to the centre of the drum to minimise energy, water and detergent consumption, and a new electronic control system. The plastic tub, spray paddles and the spin wash concept from New Wave were retained.

The resulting 'Quattro Easy Logic AA' model achieved an 'A' rating on the energy label for both energy efficiency and wash performance, compared to B and C ratings respectively for New Wave Plus 5, plus reduced water consumption.

Other models in the range, aimed at more price-sensitive market segments –a mid-price model with electromechanical controls, and a lower-priced design without the pumped recirculation system – perform better than or equal to New Wave in terms of energy and water consumption and wash performance.

The same marketing principles were adopted for another new laundry range launched in 2002. Top of the range is an electronically controlled model, Hoover Vision Plus (Figure 63), with an angled drum for easy loading. It is rated A+ for energy efficiency, A for wash performance and spin-drying and has programmes with a water consumption of just 35 litres. Other models in the range also emphasise low energy and water consumption and feature programmes to meet different user needs, such as fast washing of sports kit, low water temperature and hand washing.

Figure 63 Hoover Vision Plus washing machine in aluminium finish, in production 2002 to 2005 Source: Hoover European Appliance Group

Environmental management

After the departure of Hoover's director of engineering development, who had acted as environmental champion, the company seemed for a time to become less pro-active on environmental issues. As noted above, under Candy Group ownership, Hoover introduced the production system for the new laundry range primarily for strategic and economic reasons, rather than environmental reasons. Nevertheless, the new electrostatic powder coating plant uses no solvents and produces less waste and emissions than the wet paint plant used before introduction of the New Wave range. Packaging and transport have not changed from the systems introduced for New Wave. Hoover did not design its new machines for ease of disassembly and recycling, although all plastic components are marked as before.

The main environmental benefits arise from the greater energy efficiency and lower water consumption of the new machines compared to the ranges they replaced. As over 90% of the environmental impacts of a washing machine arise from its use, these improvements almost certainly outweigh any increases in environmental impacts arising from other parts of the life cycle.

Although for many years Hoover was the only washing machine manufacturer granted an ecolabel, like its competitors the company did not apply for an ecolabel for its new laundry ranges. Hoover considered that the energy label was more relevant, while the few marketing advantages of the ecolabel did not justify its costs.

In 2003, as part of the group's corporate social responsibility policy, Candy updated its environmental policy. Candy Group now has a number of environmental guidelines for its businesses, including:

- promoting the development of products with a limited impact on natural resources in every phase: production, use and end of life

- contributing to saving natural resources by particularly promoting the reuse and recovery of materials and energy

- privileging the use of materials having a low impact on the environment, by involving its suppliers in this process.

(http://www.candy-group.com accessed 15.2.05)

These guidelines reiterate many of the points in Hoover's environmental mission, including a commitment to life-cycle ecodesign. The effect of these guidelines on NPD at Hoover within the Candy group remains to be seen.

What else could Hoover do to reduce environmental impacts?

As you've seen, Hoover moved from a green design towards a life cycle ecodesign approach during the original New Wave project. However, it only did so after the company established its Environmental Mission and got involved in developing the EU washing machine ecolabel. By then, product development had started, so some design and manufacturing decisions already taken had to be justified retrospectively and ecodesign thinking evolved along with the product. Moreover, the company did not do everything it could to reduce the environmental impacts of its products. So, what else might a manufacturer such as Hoover have done, and what might it do in the future? Here are some possibilities for further environmental improvements of washing machines based on the some of the eight ecodesign strategies I introduced in Section 7.

Selection of low-impact materials

In addition to eliminating materials banned under EU legislation, organic solvents in cabinet coatings could be reduced or eliminated. Recycled aluminium might be used for the cabinet, so eliminating the need for coating.

Reduction of materials usage

A significant part of the weight of a washing machine is the cast iron or concrete counterweight required for stability during the spin cycle. It may be possible to use a plastics counterweight filled with water after installation, if the problem of the water stagnating could be solved (Datschefski, 1999, p.51).

Reduction of impact during use

Further reductions in the energy consumption of washing machines are technically possible, for example by improved insulation, increased motor efficiency and reduced wash temperatures. The latter measure depends on detergent formulation and consumer preferences. In some countries, use of cold-water detergents is common, while in Italy overnight wash cycles at low temperature and with minimal agitation are used. However, hot fill and hot wash options should be retained to allow use of water heated by solar panels or by renewably generated electricity.

A major source of energy consumption in washing is the use of tumble driers, so higher spin speeds that reduce the need for artificial drying are environmentally beneficial.

Many people fail to load their washing machine fully, consequently increasing energy, water and detergent consumption per kilogram of clothes washed. To help deal with this problem, some manufacturers have introduced weighing systems linked to 'fuzzy logic' controls to match the water and detergent input to suit the type, amount and dirtiness of the wash load.

Optimisation of initial lifetime

Measures that may help conserve resources and reduce waste include increasing product life, and reusing components from repaired or discarded machines. One German manufacturer designs its washing machines for a 15 to 20-year life. Although there are environmental advantages in designing products to last longer, designing for a longer life may not be beneficial due to continuing improvements in environmental performance. There are barriers to taking back and reusing components because the industry argues that such components would be outdated and unacceptable to consumers. Nevertheless, some German companies are taking back, refurbishing or remanufacturing components.

Another approach to product life extension is to design a basic chassis, which could be 'upgraded' with the latest control and motor technology at the end of its initial life. Some machines can already be reprogrammed when new detergents or wash cycles are introduced. However, the adoption by manufacturers of ecodesign approaches such as these depends on cost and market acceptability, or the introduction of new patterns of ownership, such as renting.

Optimisation of end of life system

Hoover reduced the variety of different plastics in its washing machines and marked plastic components to facilitate recycling. Although most of the steel from discarded washing machines is recycled, plastic components are usually land-filled rather than recycled. Similarly, Hoover only recovered a small proportion of packaging from distributors for recycling. However, under EC WEEE legislation, white goods manufacturers are setting up recycling schemes, in collaboration with other organisations such as local authorities and recycling companies.

Exercise 7   Lessons of the New Wave project

Look back over the washing machines case study. What lessons about product development and designing for the environment did you learn from the case study of the New Wave and its successors?

Consider:

(a) the drivers that initiated the projects

(b) environmental versus other product attributes in market success

(c) the process and organisation of NPD

(d) the organisational learning involved

(e) the extent to which these projects represented a green design or an ecodesign approach.

Spend 15–20 minutes on this exercise before looking at the discussion below.

Discussion

(a) Drivers for NPD

The factors that led to the original New Wave project included technical, market and environmental pressures and opportunities:

- loss of market share of existing Hoover washing machine ranges
- a need to replace ageing production equipment
- the introduction of 'greener' washing machines by rival manufacturers
- the prospect of environmental regulation on domestic appliances
- the presence of an environmental champion at board level.

Following the takeover by Candy, products were developed in response to new market, technical and environmental factors, including:

- the need to reduce costs and improve reliability of Hoover products
- the wish to rationalise production methods across the Candy Group
- competitive pressures for 'A' ratings on the energy label.

(b) Factors in product success

Any successful greener product must balance environmental performance against the many other design attributes wanted by the market at which the product is aimed, and do so at a competitive price. Studies of the New Wave and other greener products have shown that, to be commercially successful, they have to be competitive in terms of performance, quality and value for money before environmental friendliness enters the list of customer requirements (ENDS, 1996).

(c) Process and organisation of NPD

Incorporating environmental objectives into the NPD process does not require a fundamental change to that process. However, it's vital that this process is organised and carried out in an integrated manner. Moving towards a concurrent, cross-functional team-based approach for New Wave meant that from the planning stage onwards team members considered the marketing, engineering/industrial design, production and financial aspects of the product. Although some environmental criteria were included from the beginning of NPD, others were only introduced retrospectively and the team 'learned as it went along'. After New Wave concurrent engineering was taken further with smaller, more closely integrated, product development teams, more parallel working and computerised project management.

(d) Learning about design for the environment

For most companies, designing for the environment is a new activity and so will require a learning process. Such organisational learning depends on the commitment of senior management. When Hoover began the New Wave project, the choice of materials and production processes was mainly determined by performance, cost and efficiency considerations. The design focus was on energy and water consumption. With a board member acting as environmental champion, Hoover introduced its Environmental Mission, and got involved in the EU ecolabelling scheme, As a result, Hoover attempted to assess and reduce environmental impacts throughout the New Wave's life cycle. In other words, during the project Hoover moved from a green design approach towards a life cycle ecodesign approach.

Although environmental policy seems to have had less emphasis after Candy's takeover, Hoover's machines and production processes continued to improve environmentally. Candy Group then reiterated its commitment to an environmental policy and life-cycle ecodesign. Nevertheless, consideration of possible ecodesign strategies indicates that there is considerably more that washing machine manufacturers could do to reduce the environmental impacts of their products.

Key points of Section 8

- Ecodesign projects do not involve any significant changes to the NPD process: environmental objectives simply introduce another element into the product design specification for the designer or design team to take into account during product development.

- Ecodesign projects should involve concurrent engineering and be organised via a dedicated cross-functional team, or a matrix structure, to integrate environmental expertise from the beginning of NPD.

- Integrating ecodesign into NPD is an organisational learning process that takes time and depends on management commitment and the development of an environmental policy.

- There is usually much more that could be done to reduce the environmental impacts of products by applying life cycle ecodesign strategies, but implementation depends on overcoming cost, market and other constraints.

9 Sustainable design and innovation

9.1 Limits of ecodesign

Although ecodesign strategies can reduce the environmental impacts of existing products, like green design, ecodesign has limitations. As you saw in Section 7, ecodesign may reduce the life-cycle environmental impacts of a product compared to previous ones by up to 50% (factor 2) in the short term and perhaps up to 80% (factor 5) after 10 years of successive improvement. But reducing the impacts of individual products by such amounts will not be enough to deal with the environmental problems posed by increasing global levels of production and consumption.

It has been estimated that to allow the growing populations of developing countries to reach acceptable living standards, while moving towards an ecologically sustainable world, will require reducing energy and resource consumption, and pollution generated per head in the industrialised countries during the twenty-first century, by anything from 75% (factor 4) to 95% (factor 20). A target that is often quoted by the United Nations Environment Programme is a 90% (or factor 10) reduction (UNEP, 1999, p. 12). The UK government has already adopted a target of reducing climate-changing carbon emissions by 60% from 1990 levels by 2050, and is committed under the Kyoto Protocol to reduce its total greenhouse gas emissions by 12.5% in the period 2008–2012.

Although ecodesign can contribute to reducing energy/resource consumption and emissions, the scale of the challenge has led to the concepts of sustainable design and sustainable innovation. I mentioned these approaches earlier as '@ new concept development' in the ecodesign strategy wheel and I'll discuss them in more detail in this section.

9.2 Sustainable design

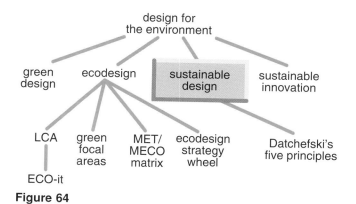

Figure 64

9.2.1 Principles of sustainable design

Sustainable design (Figure 64) can mean taking ecodesign to its limits, as Datschefski (2001) has proposed with his five principles of a sustainable product. Datschefski says a sustainable product should first address the materials, energy and toxic emissions and waste (MET) issues as follows:

(M) *cyclic* – the product is made from compostable, organic materials or from minerals that are continuously recycled in a closed loop

(E) *solar* – the product in manufacture and use consumes only renewable energy that is cyclic and safe

(T) *safe* – all releases to air, water, land or space are 'food' for other systems.

In addition, Datschefski says to be fully sustainable a product should also be:

efficient – requiring 90% less energy, materials and water than products providing equivalent utility did in 1990

social – its manufacture and use supports basic human rights and natural justice.

(Datschefski, 2001, p. 29)

Datschefski admits that very few products fully meet his five ideal principles of sustainable design. However, he gives examples of existing products and buildings that would help him to live a 'sustainable day'. In this day, he wakes to the sun warming his solar-heated and wind-powered home; drinks organic, fair-trade tea while listening to his human-powered wind-up radio, then discards the teabag into the worm composter; dons a fleece made from recycled plastic bottles before driving to work in his bio-diesel-fuelled car. And so on ...

Datschefski (p. 73) notes that although none of his 'sustainable day' products are '100% cyclic, solar and safe', they do go a long way to reducing the environmental and social impacts of daily life.

On the T307 DVD, Edwin Datschefski talks about the importance of life-cycle thinking in design and the principles of sustainable products. You should already have viewed this sequence during your study of the *Invention and innovation* block. If not, you should do so at a convenient point during your study of this section.

9.2.2 Green function innovation

A less idealistic view of sustainable design is one in which the *function* of the product is considered and alternative, environmentally sustainable technical means for providing it are examined.

For example, instead of redesigning a refrigerator, washing machine or tumble drier, the designer attempts to apply a technology that is environmentally optimal, to provide the essential functions of preserving fresh food or cleaning and drying clothes. Hence, this approach is sometimes called 'green function innovation'.

Sustainable products that provide existing functions in new technical ways are mostly still at the R&D stage or are just concept or prototype designs. For example, as a sustainable design training project, a team

Figure 65 Prototype solar-powered clothes-drying cupboard. The cupboard is built into the wall and connected to a solar panel on the outside of the building that provides warm air that is blown into the cupboard.

of designers from Electrolux and Cranfield University developed several concepts for an 'EcoKitchen' competition, including a zero-energy fridge based on passive cooling (Thompson and Sherwin, 2001, p. 360). A Dutch design consultancy has designed a prototype solar-powered clothes drier, comprising an insulated cupboard connected to a solar panel that provides warm air driven by a small electric fan through the cupboard. The device uses much less power than a tumble drier and, with few moving parts, should last longer (Figure 65).

However, a well-known example of what is arguably a sustainable design, which was developed beyond the prototype to the production and marketing stages, was the original Freeplay wind-up radio. Let's examine this example a bit more closely.

Case study Freeplay wind-up radio

The Freeplay radio invented by Trevor Baylis is often hailed as a sustainable design because it satisfies the three pillars of sustainability: *social*, *environmental* and *economic*. The clockwork mechanism eliminates the need for mains electricity or batteries (environmental), and meets educational and health (social) and employment (economic) needs in a developing country. Nevertheless, Baylis originally created the radio for social rather than environmental or economic reasons.

In 1991, Baylis saw a TV documentary about AIDS in Africa and learned that radio was often the only means of education that could help reduce the spread of AIDS, but the need for batteries or electricity made radio access expensive or difficult. That night, he got the idea for a wind-up radio and the next day made a mock-up to test his idea – an electric motor turned in reverse by a hand brace to act as a dynamo, connected to an old transistor radio. Baylis went on to design a prototype clockwork radio that played for 14 minutes with a two-minute wind (Figure 66). He applied for a patent (Figure 66) and approached potential manufacturers, none of whom were interested.

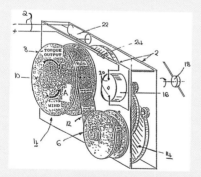

Figure 66 Patent drawing of clockwork radio, filed 1991. The constant force spring that drives the dynamo is the band of steel wound onto spools. Source: Patent GB 2262324

Fortunately, as a result of demonstrating the prototype on the BBC TV programme 'Tomorrow's World', a South African accountant, Chris Staines, saw the programme, recognised the potential of such a radio, and visited Baylis with a business proposal. Staines and a business partner then went to Africa to research the market and get reactions to the prototype (market research, see the *Markets* block). The battery-free prototype interested potential users, but to satisfy the African market it would have to be bigger and play longer and louder.

The partners managed to get funding from a South African foundation for product development with the aim of establishing a manufacturing plant in Cape Town that would employ disabled people. A consortium, including manufacturers, a university engineering department, and a firm of design consultants, turned the prototype into a marketable product.

The original Freeplay radio (Figure 67) was launched in 1995 and was very successful, selling around the world. However, after a few years, the company that employed disabled people in South Africa to make Freeplay human-powered products decided for economic reasons to shift production to China. The clockwork technology of the original Freeplay radio was also abandoned in favour of a lighter and more efficient system of using human and/or solar power to recharge batteries (Figure 68), and the target market became Western consumers, backpackers, and so on rather than rural Africans.

The new range of Freeplay radios (one of which is shown in Figure 68) therefore lacks the 'social' element of sustainable design of the original, although they still offer environmental advantages over conventional portable radios.

(a)

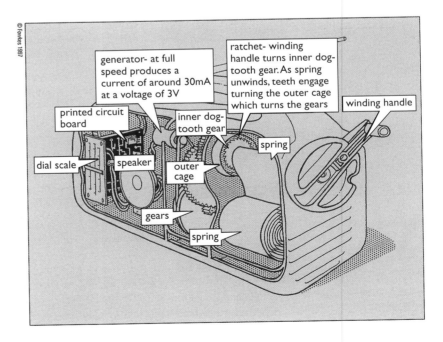

(b)

Figure 67   (a) Original Freeplay wind-up radio made in South Africa by disabled workers. (b) Components and operating principle of the original Freeplay radio. Source: (b) Chick, 1997, p. 55

(a)

(b)

Figure 68 Freeplay Ranger radio with batteries recharged by human or solar power, or a mains adapter, and made in China Source: Freeplay Group

9.2.3 Sustainable design at Philips

Let's look next at a multinational business that since the early 1990s has increasingly integrated ecodesign into its product development activities as part of its environmental policy and has begun to adopt sustainable design and sustainable innovation as part of a new sustainability policy.

Case study | Corporate sustainability at Philips

Royal Philips Electronics is one of the world's major manufacturers of lighting, electronics, electrical and medical equipment. It is also one of the leading multinationals in adopting ecodesign and sustainability as an integral part of its corporate strategy. Philips is an early member of the World Business Council for Sustainable Development (WBCSD), a coalition of many international companies committed to 'sustainable development via the three pillars of economic growth, ecological balance and social progress' formed as the business response to the 1992 United Nations Conference on Environment and Development (Rio Earth Summit) (Schmidheiney, 1992).

Sustainability policy

Philips released its sustainability policy in 2002, but the policy had evolved over many years, starting with the company's environmental performance guidelines formulated in 1970 and its global environmental policy first issued in 1987 and updated in 1991. Philips sustainability policy states;

> Sustainable development [which the policy defines as the 'simultaneous pursuit of economic prosperity, environmental quality and social equity'] is a priority for the board of management ... With its tradition of integrating economic, environmental and social issues, Philips understands that sustainable development is one of the most challenging issues facing the world.

> (Philips, 2005, p. 90)

Philips sees sustainability as comprising the following three responsibilities (these are the three pillars of sustainability, sometimes known as the 'triple bottom line' or 'people, planet, profit'):

Economic

This responsibility means ensuring sustained and profitable growth in a rapidly changing global economy. This is the key element of Philips' corporate strategy, via which it aims to grow over the next few years from a €30 billion to a €50 billion business. This strategy is based on providing 'solutions' (new products, technical innovations and services) that improve peoples' quality of life in the key areas of health, lifestyle and enabling technology for markets in the developed and, increasingly, the developing world (Figure 69). The company views meeting its social and environmental responsibilities as contributing to its economic success. As Philips' *Sustainability Report 2004* says:

> It is our firm belief that socially and environmentally responsible behaviour contributes to sustained profitable growth and value creation. That's why we are embedding sustainability thinking and acting in all of our daily activities. This is our philosophy and a cornerstone of our strategy.

(Philips, 2005, p. 24)

Figure 69   Relationship of Philips' philosophy of sustainability to its corporate strategy Source: Philips, 2005, p. 24

Social

Within Philips itself, social responsibility means many things, including designing products that meet customer needs, ensuring safe working conditions, involving employees in decision making, and providing retraining for those made redundant by restructuring. Externally, it means, for example, requiring Philips' suppliers to adhere to minimum standards of health and safety and to avoid the use of child labour. It also means supporting social and community activities, such as educational and health projects, across the world.

Environmental

This responsibility means minimising the depletion of resources and harmful impacts on the environment resulting from the manufacture and supply of Philips products, services and technologies.

I'll look next in a bit more detail at how Philips tries to meet its environmental responsibilities.

Environmental programmes and ecodesign

Philips' environmental policy has evolved since the early 1990s from a primary focus on end-of-pipe cleanup of manufacturing processes and single-issue green design projects – such as reducing hazardous substances in consumer electronic products – to an established ecodesign process. Since 2002, the company has made moves towards sustainable design and innovation, as discussed below (Caluwe, 2004).

The company's systematic approach to environmental improvement began with the 1994 Environmental Opportunity Programme, followed by three 'EcoVision' programmes from 1998–2001, 2002–2005 and 2006–2009. These programmes set targets to Philips' five product divisions for environmental improvements to both products and manufacturing processes, and introduced ecodesign principles into the product creation (NPD) process (Figure 70).

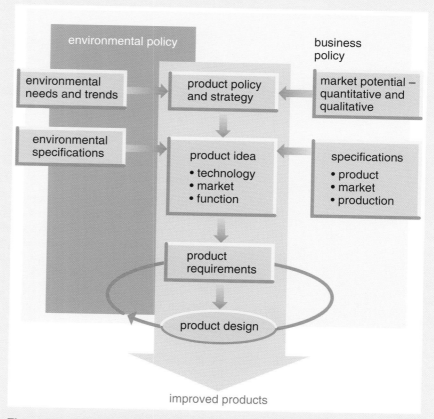

Figure 70 Environmental and business inputs to the product creation process within Philips' environmental opportunities programme
Source: Philips, c. 1996

Progress of each division towards the targets is measured on Philips' ecodesign maturity grid. For example, under the 'EcoVision 2002–5' programme, all product divisions are required to reduce their manufacturing energy consumption by 10% by 2005 and should aim for a 20% reduction. Likewise, product creation teams in the product divisions (such as Consumer Electronics) and their associated business groups (such as Television), plus Philips Design, are required to apply approved ecodesign procedures in all projects by 2005. This is because the different divisions and businesses evolved different methods and are at different levels of commitment to ecodesign. In Philips Lighting, for example, ecodesign is more advanced than in the Domestic Appliances and Personal Care division.

Green focal areas

However, despite the differences in ecodesign maturity, all design teams are expected to focus on one or more of five green focal areas (Figure 71) when creating new or improved products:

- reduction in *weight*
- reduction or elimination of *hazardous substances*
- minimising *energy consumption*
- increased *recycling* and reduced *disposal*
- reduction, reuse, recycling of *packaging*.

weight   hazardous substances   energy consumption   recycling and disposal   packaging

Figure 71 Green focal areas focus the attention of product development teams at Philips Source: Philips, 2005, p. 60

As noted in Section 7, Philips adopted this simple checklist approach to embedding ecodesign throughout the business after some divisions had tried using more complex LCA-based methods. The green focal areas have proved to be a practical ecodesign approach usable by designers across the organisation. Design teams that are motivated to go further are encouraged to use LCA tools – an example being EcoScan software, which is similar to ECO-it – that Philips Medical Systems uses for ecodesign.

With experience, Philips discovered that the green focal areas differ in importance for different products. For example, lifetime is important for lighting products as longer life saves both costs and materials. In 2004, therefore, the lighting division introduced 'lifetime' as a new focal area. For consumer electronic products, reducing packaging size and weight, to lower the costs and impacts of transport and distribution, is of particular concern.

So, while attempting to address all the focal areas, different divisions and businesses often concentrate on particular ones – for example the use of recycled material for packaging. Sometimes, this has resulted in what is essentially single-issue green design rather than ecodesign proper. All businesses have, of course, to address areas covered by legislation, such as eliminating certain hazardous substances and providing for product take-back and recycling required by the WEEE directive. The lighting division, for example, has made major efforts to reduce the mercury content of fluorescent lamps to the required levels or better and to establish a system for take-back and recycling of its lamps.

Green flagships

Under EcoVision, each product division is also required to develop at least one so-called 'green flagship' product per year. These products offer quantitatively-measured better environmental performance than their predecessors, or closest competitors, in two or more green focal areas. Not surprisingly, divisions with the most-developed ecodesign procedures produced the most green flagships. The lighting division, for example, developed eight green flagship products in 2004, including the ALTO Energy Advantage fluorescent lamp (Figure 72a).

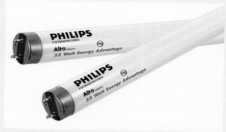

(a)

(b)

(c)

Figure 72 Some of Philips' green flagships. (a) ALTO Energy Advantage 25 W fluorescent lamp. (b) 32PF9956 flat TV, which uses less energy and needs less packaging. (c) The PCA2002U/10 watch circuit weighs less, is free of hazardous substances, uses less energy and needs less packaging compared with its predecessor. Source: Philips, 2005, pp. 63–65

Consumer Electronics also developed eight green flagship products in 2004, including a DVD player, a digital music player and a large flat-screen TV (Figure 72b).

Philips Domestic Appliances and Personal Care only managed one green flagship product in 2004, the Azur Precise iron with a novel steam tip. Compared with the average of its closest competitors, the iron weighs 5% less and the environmental impact of its packaging is 59% less.

Philips Semiconductors also produced one green flagship product in 2003/4 – a family of watch circuits with the lowest power consumption on the market and programmable to any modern watch motor (Figure 72c).

As you can see, Philips' ecodesign methods have taken years to evolve, sometimes produce only single-issue green designs, and have still to fully diffuse throughout a large organisation. As one Philips insider notes:

> Over the course of almost 15 years, the application of eco-design within Philips ... has grown from an 'ad hoc' activity, driven by green champions, to an integrated part of all the Philips business units' product creation processes. Environmental aspects may not be a driving factor in Philips product development ... however, driven by the Philips environmental programme EcoVision II, all project teams must at least give some thought to the environmental targets set for their business and relevant to their product. Furthermore, to keep in line with ... increased outsourcing and co-development, the Philips' supply chain is introduced to green requirements .... Of course, there is room for improvement, as Philips has not yet reached all the targets as set by the EcoVision program, and to reach them, it will still need to keep working at it.
>
> (Caluwe, 2004, p. 220)

Sustainable design

Since 2004, the EcoVision programme has included social as well as environmental targets for product development. This is mainly achieved via the company's management policies for external product manufacturers and component suppliers:

> Philips' supplier declaration on sustainability outlines the minimum expectations of behaviour in the areas of environment, health and safety, and labour conditions, including child and forced labour. Adhering to these requirements ... has become an important factor in the company's decision to maintain business relationships.
>
> (Philips 2005, p. 80)

Under EcoVision, therefore, Philips is beginning to move from ecodesign towards socially and environmentally responsible sustainable design.

Sustainable business initiatives

Within its sustainability policy, Philips views the markets of the newly industrialised and developing world as both an economic opportunity to grow the business and as a way to meet its social and environmental responsibilities.

Philips' *Sustainability Report 2004* states:

> Our challenge lies in expanding our scope to new markets and new business opportunities with sustainability as a key driver. This includes new business models that will allow us to contribute in a meaningful and sustainable way to the quality of life of the 4 billion people of the world at the bottom of the economic pyramid, who earn less than US$1500 a year.
>
> (Philips, 2005, p. 19)

To start the process of opening up new markets in the developing world, Philips asked its employees to come up with innovative business ideas that address the needs of the poor. All of these pilot sustainable business initiatives involve partnerships between local Philips businesses and other organisations, and involve innovations in both products and services.

The company is especially concerned to bridge the 'digital divide' between the developed and developing world in access to information and communications technologies. This has led to pilot sustainable innovation projects, including the following begun in 2004 (Philips, 2005, pp. 31–34; Philips, 2006, pp. 20–25).

Voices-in-your-hand project in Brazil

This project, by Philips Latin America in partnership with World Vision and other organisations, aims to bring digital connectivity to people in the slums of Recife, Brazil. Individuals or families – many of whom are illiterate – can communicate with others and have access to information, even though fixed-line or mobile phones are beyond their reach. People can listen to personalised webcasts of audio information offline in their homes, talk back and use voice email using modified MP3 players (Figure 73). To link their sets to the internet, they visit a public utility point. The pilot concluded in 2005 and less costly approaches for scaling up the service as a new business are being investigated.

Figure 73 Philips' voices-in-your-hand pilot project brings the internet to a poor community in Brazil by using modified MP3 players, allowing people to communicate with others and have access to information
Source: Philips, 2005, p. 33

Wind-up radios for villagers in India

The Philips innovation campus in Bangalore, India, launched a pilot project in June 2004 to sell Philips products in villages. Philips India wind-up radios, launched in 2002, were already selling in substantial numbers. Together with a community development organisation, the project team used the services of financial self-help groups (SHG) to help sell the radios. As many rural villages have electrical power for only one or two hours a day, wind-up radios offer a way to get news, music and crop prices without the cost of batteries. The SHG, aided by loans provided by Philips and its employees, quickly sold 200 wind-up radios to villagers at about £8 (approx. €13) payable in instalments, thus enabling the loans to be repaid. A scaled-up pilot is planned during 2005 including more regions in India, as well as a more extensive product range to meet villagers' aspirations.

Distant healthcare advancement in India

Philips India has developed a business plan for providing distance healthcare for the poor. Called DISHA (distance healthcare advancement), this project aims to deliver diagnostics to those who are not served by the existing healthcare system. The company conducted research in target communities to determine the best means of delivery, which also resulted in a focus on two key areas – mother and child, and trauma.

Philips India formed partnerships with hospitals and volunteer doctors, satellite communications providers and a community development organisation in order to advance the project, while Philips customised a 'tele-clinical' van with diagnostic equipment to launch the project in 2005. The project was expanded in 2006 with the aim of establishing DISHA as a commercial new business.

New technologies

While aiming to expand its businesses to the markets of the newly industrialised and developing world, sometimes with lower-cost versions of its existing products, Philips still sells most of its products in developed countries and is constantly researching, designing and developing innovative technologies and products aimed initially at those markets.

An important innovation that should satisfy both the economic and environmental pillars of sustainability is LED (light-emitting diode) lighting. LED lighting is much more energy efficient and longer lasting than existing fluorescent or incandescent lamps. LED lighting can be embedded in other products such as furniture (see the cover of this book) and computer controlled to change colour and brightness. Philips has a range of LED lighting systems, initially intended mainly for use in shops and hotels, and has various R&D and design projects to develop and exploit the potential of this and other new sustainable technologies.

Balancing the pillars of sustainability

Philips' senior management does not consider its economic responsibility of ensuring profitable growth of its business from €30 to €50 billion to be in conflict with the company's social and environmental responsibilities. Nevertheless, since 2003 the company seems to have shifted from aiming *simultaneously* to satisfy its economic, social and environmental responsibilities to that of attempting to *balance* the 'sometimes-competing' demands of integrating those responsibilities.

Therefore, Philips' *Sustainability Report 2004* states:

> We continue to be dedicated to sustainability, to finding the proper balance between the sometimes-competing demands of integrating social, environmental and economic responsibility. To do that, we are working to embed sustainability thinking in all of our day-to-day operations.
>
> (Philips, 2005, p. 16)

So, Philips now recognises that pursuing economic growth may sometimes conflict with its social and/or environmental responsibilities. In such a large organisation, there are of course differing views on how to achieve sustainability. Nevertheless, senior managers in the company consider that technological innovation should enable Philips to grow profitably and responsibly by supplying its products, services and technology to improve the quality of life of the world's population without irretrievably damaging the environment or running out of resources.

For example, Henk de Bruin, head of Philips' corporate sustainability office, says:

> ... being a technology-driven company, we think that technology will provide, in most of the cases, a solution ... sustainability means that we have, currently, four billion people living at the bottom of the pyramid ... they want to get to the same level of welfare as you and I. Some people ... think we have to go down a level in order for them to go up. That never will happen ... we will maintain our level, or a higher level and they will try to accelerate and also get to the same level. I am an optimist, I think that technology ... of course in the proper political framework, will provide a solution.
>
> (de Bruin, 2005 'Talking Innovation' on the T307 DVD)

Conclusion

Philips is a company at the forefront of corporate strategy on sustainability, environmental management and design for the environment. It is still learning and working to embed its environmental improvement programme throughout the organisation, and having to face the difficulties of balancing the pursuit of economic growth and profit with its social and environmental responsibilities within its strategy of sustainable development.

You can learn more about Philips' approach to sustainability and ecodesign on the video 'Philips: design for sustainability' on the T307 DVD. If you have not yet viewed it and the associated course team comments, do so at a convenient time when studying this section and then attempt the following SAQs.

SAQ 11

(a) What led Philips to adopt a sustainability policy?

(b) What is Philips' strategy for growth within its sustainability policy?

SAQ 12

(a) How does Philips attempt to meet its environmental responsibilities within its sustainability policy?

(b) How is the company embedding ecodesign into the product creation process?

SAQ 13

Why does Philips believe it can grow economically while still being socially and environmentally sustainable?

9.3 Sustainable innovation

Sustainable innovation (Figure 74) is broader in scope than sustainable design, and goes beyond technical solutions, as in the pilot new business initiatives described in the Philips case study. In sustainable innovation, a team develops new, environmentally optimum mixes of products and services, or socio-technical systems, to provide a required function such as clean clothes, warmth or mobility.

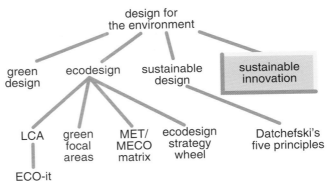

Figure 74

Sustainable innovation involves moving from the design of individual products to the design of whole systems, and so is sometimes called green system innovation. The long-term aim is to achieve the 90% or more (factor 10 or greater) reduction in energy and resource consumption per head in the industrialised world required for global sustainability. Sustainable innovation aims to achieve the reduction by greater eco-efficiency and changes in consumption patterns rather than less consumption.

Exercise 8   Green system innovation

What different systems can you think of to provide the function of cleaning crockery, cutlery and cooking utensils for a household of, say, two adults and two children? The systems can comprise different mixes of people, products, and/or services and should be based on available technologies. Which system(s) are likely to have the lowest environmental impacts?

Spend 10 minutes making notes on this exercise before looking at the discussion below.

Discussion

You might have listed the following systems of people, products and services to provide this function.

- Washing up by hand with liquid detergent and water heated by gas or fossil fuel generated electricity.

- Washing up using a standard, or an ecodesigned, dishwasher, supplied with dishwasher detergent and rinse aid, and salt for water softening.

- A combination of hand washing up (e.g. of pots and pans) and use of a dishwasher.

- Washing up by hand with a 'green' liquid detergent and water heated by solar panels and/or electricity generated from renewable sources.

- Washing up using a dishwasher hot filled by water from solar panels and/or powered by electricity generated from renewable sources and using a 'green' dishwasher detergent and vinegar as a rinse aid.

- Employing someone to do the washing up by hand and/or dishwasher.

- Use of disposable plates and cutlery, combined with hand washing up and/or dishwashing.

- A dishwashing service equipped with commercial dishwashing equipment.

Without a life-cycle assessment study, it is difficult to be certain which of the above systems is likely to have the lowest environmental impacts. One such study showed that washing up more than nine place settings by hand with water heated by gas uses more energy than a dishwasher. Similarly, washing up more than three place settings by hand consumed more water than using a dishwasher (DEFRA, 2004). Therefore, using a fully loaded dishwasher with solar-heated water or powered by renewable electricity and using a 'green' dishwasher detergent is likely to be the system with lowest environmental impacts.

As well as new mixes of products and services, such as a dishwasher powered by 'green' electricity, sustainable innovation can involve new patterns of ownership, such as leasing, that allow the return of a product to its manufacturer for refurbishing or upgrading. It might involve more radical changes, such as a shared or communal use of products, for example car-sharing schemes (discussed in the *Consumption* block). It might even involve replacing physical products, such as CDs, with a 'dematerialised' service, for example internet-delivered music files. Such new ownership patterns often also involve technological innovations, and vice versa.

Sustainable innovation in transport systems, for instance, is likely to involve changing from private cars to improved public transport systems, car-sharing schemes and environmentally benign forms, such as hybrid petrol–electric vehicles and bicycles. Sustainable innovation may also involve questioning whether the product or function is really needed. For example, designing a sustainable transport system raises the question of whether to curb the growing demand for travel, or whether some travel might be replaced by electronic communication.

The following case study describes a small-scale sustainable transport system involving innovations in both products and services or organisation; described in Part 1 as configurational innovations. As I noted in Part 1, the development process for product–service systems is essentially the same as that for manufactured products but, as in this case, often involves many partner organisations and therefore requires more complex management and co-ordination.

Case study   ASTI PlusBus service

In the late 1990s, the European Commission provided financial support for demonstration projects of innovative green transport technologies. As part of this scheme, Camden Community Transport in London was awarded a grant to purchase and operate a fleet of three electric and three compressed natural gas (CNG) minibuses. On their own, such cleaner-fuelled vehicles are essentially 'green designs', but this project took a systems design approach that moved the service towards becoming a sustainable innovation.

The community transport sector provides specialist transport for people with reduced mobility, such as the elderly and people with disabilities. Often such services are provided by separate organisations (for example the Red Cross and health authorities). Users book trips on each provider, depending on whether they are going, say, to a day centre or hospital appointment. Typically, the minibus undertakes a lengthy trip to pick up or drop all passengers to/from their home.

The ASTI project sought not only to provide greener vehicles, but also to redesign the system by integrating the (often poor) services provided by these different organisations, with particular attention to sustainability. This would produce a new product–service mix that was better for users and, through using the fleet of existing and greener vehicles more efficiently, result in reduced environmental impacts. This product–service synthesis was reflected in the project's title of ASTI (accessible sustainable transport integration). The design specification for ASTI was therefore that of the service rather than the technical performance of the greener vehicles.

New satellite vehicle tracking and trip allocation software for realtime service optimisation and trip scheduling was crucial to creating the new product–service mix. Instead of running five or six separate minibus services, they were all combined into a single service called PlusBus, with the providers pooling their vehicle fleets. This produced a considerably better service to users. Someone, for example, waiting to go to a hospital appointment, would now be taken on a Council Social Services bus that was in the area at the right time, whereas before it might have driven past their door with only one person on board.

However, the costs and revenues in this shared operation need to be allocated to the different providers. This required sophisticated computer software that would allocate the costs and revenues between the partners in the scheme. The software would also need to group trip requests as they come in, so as to make the best use of the bus capacity.

A key result of the ASTI study was that the technical challenge of the project was not about the electric and CNG minibuses, but the development of this real-time trip, cost and revenue allocation software. Furthermore, the reduction in energy use, pollution and CO_2 emissions from the integration of the separate services was much greater than from introducing the high-profile greener vehicles. One important lesson that came out from this study was that such a sustainable innovation approach requires more complex and co-operative management compared to a green or ecodesign approach. It would have been organisationally easier for all the separate operators to buy their own electric or CNG minibuses, but the environmental improvements would have been relatively small and users would have continued to have a poor transport service.

(This case study was prepared by Stephen Potter, based on Potter, 1999)

There is evidence of growing government and business interest in such product and service innovations needed to move towards sustainability. For example, the UK government's Sustainable Development Strategy (DEFRA, 2005, p. 67), stated that:

Service innovation ... can offer potential efficiency gains ... If suppliers ... supply a service, rather than a product ... opportunities for profit and reductions in resource use are created. An energy supplier could shift from selling energy to providing a warm home service. The approach is based on aligning the incentives of customer and supplier. Both can gain from cost reductions derived from improved resource efficiency.

A major Netherlands government programme on sustainable technology development examined systems innovations to achieve up to 95% (factor 20) reductions in environmental impacts. In a book on the findings of this programme, Weaver et al (2000, p. 20) state:

> ... sustainable technologies will most often consist of path-breaking approaches to meeting needs that are radically different from the solutions we have in place today .... Sustainable technologies would be ones capable of meeting 'needs' using only a fraction of the 'eco-capacity' ... used by today's technologies.

I shall consider sustainable innovation in more detail in this section, again using the example of washing machines, but this time thinking beyond product design to consider the design of a more sustainable system for the provision of clean clothes.

Case study | Sustainable innovation in clothing care

As you've seen, sustainable innovation involves considering whether a product's essential functions might be performed by an alternative socio-technical system that produces lower environment impacts. How might you apply this strategic approach to the design of a more sustainable system of clothing care?

Innovations in clothes-cleaning technology

First, I'll consider what might be done through innovations in design and technology to achieve a more sustainable clothing care system.

There has been active R&D on washing machine technology for some years: many patents exist and there are several designs at prototype stage, or in production, that significantly reduce water and detergent consumption. For example, the Japanese company, Sanyo, has developed machines that use two new technologies. Its ultrasonic washing machine produces millions of tiny air bubbles whose breakdown causes ultrasonic waves, allowing the bubbles to penetrate the clothes' fibres to clean them with less detergent (Figure 75a). Sanyo's 'open drum' machine electrolyses the water to produce active oxygen and hypochlorite ions to clean and deodorise clothes. A design that combines ultrasonic with electrolysing technologies that cleans lightly soiled clothes without the need for detergent was launched in Japan in 2002 (Figure 75b).

(a)

(b)

Figure 75 New washing machine technologies. (a) Sanyo ultrasonic ASW-U108T produces air bubbles that penetrate the clothes' fibres to clean them with less detergent. (b) Sanyo open drum AWD-A845Z electrolyses the water to clean and deodorise clothes. Sources: (a) http://www.global-sanyo.com/product/index.html accessed 20.3.05; (b) *Triz Journal*

In addition, the use of renewable energy to power washing machines and to heat water, together with new low-temperature detergents, could offer equal or greater environmental improvements than those offered by new washing machine technologies.

Innovations in ownership of clothes-cleaning equipment

Second, let's consider changes in the ownership of clothes-cleaning equipment that might lead to the development of a more sustainable clothing care system. These include (Ryan, 2004, pp. 58–59):

● A system of leasing rather than direct purchase of washing machines to enable consumers to return their machines to manufacturers for recycling, or for upgrading to incorporate the latest technology. (Recycling of electrical equipment is required anyway under WEEE legislation. The latter is similar to renting a television set, which after a period is returned for replacement with an upgraded machine.)

● A system in which consumers have a contract with a service company that provides a home washing machine and records the energy supply for operating the machine. The consumer pays per use of the machine and the service company maintains, upgrades and recycles the machines. (This has similarities to the 'pay-as-you-go' system for some mobile phones.)

● Communal or commercial laundry facilities equipped with the most environmentally efficient clothes-cleaning technologies.

The Netherlands government's sustainable technology development programme sponsored research on sustainable clothes washing up to 2025 and beyond (van den Hoed, 1997; Weaver et al, 2002, pp. 171–203). The project examined whether a 95% (factor 20) improvement in 'eco-efficiency' could be achieved through technical innovation alone or through a shift from individually owned products to shared services. The shared services considered were a small neighbourhood wash centre and a large commercial laundry. The measures of eco-efficiency for all three scenarios were the amounts of primary energy, water and detergent consumed per kilogram of washed clothes.

The study indicated that improvements in household washing technology (e.g., low-temperature detergents and sensors to optimise machine loading) could produce a 60% (factor 2.5) reduction in energy consumption by 2025. The neighbourhood wash centre or large laundry could achieve some 55% reductions in energy consumption by 2025 through use of renewable sources, combined heat and power and improved machines. The shared services produced similar reductions in energy consumption to those at the household level, because some energy savings in laundries are offset by the need for higher wash temperatures, more artificial drying and fuel for transport. In addition, due to the efficiencies of scale and availability of skilled operators, the large laundry service could achieve 90% (factor 10) reductions in water consumption and detergent use by 2025, through measures such as water and detergent recycling, compared to 20–33% reductions for the household and neighbourhood systems. Therefore, about 60% reductions in energy per unit of service offered (in this case, per kg of clean clothes) were achievable in all three scenarios. But none of the systems managed to achieve the desired 95% reductions in environmental impacts, although the large laundry offered 90% reductions in water and detergent use by 2025. In the longer term, the study concludes, laundries could probably offer greater eco-efficiency improvements by use of new technologies, such as ultrasonic cleaning, mentioned earlier.

However, the study also recognised that there are major barriers in persuading people to shift to eco-efficient neighbourhood wash centres or laundries unless the cost and convenience was similar or better than home clothes washing.

New patterns of clothes ownership and care

If changing the technology and ownership of clothes-cleaning equipment cannot achieve 90% or greater reductions in environmental impacts, perhaps changes to the way clothing is produced and consumed could. The SusHouse material on the T307 DVD contains five future scenarios about radical changes to the production, ownership and cleaning of clothes that could drastically reduce the environmental impacts of clothing care by 2050.

SusHouse method

The development of long-term future scenarios for three household functions – Clothing care, Shelter and Food – were part of a major EU-funded project called The Sustainable Household (SusHouse), which built on the methods developed in the Dutch sustainable technology development programme mentioned above (Green and Vergracht, 2002). For the clothing care function, creativity workshops were held in Italy, The Netherlands and Germany in which producers, consumers, technical experts, and government representatives brainstormed ideas for sustainable futures for the production, consumption and care of clothing in the year 2050. From the brainstorming sessions, the SusHouse project team constructed five so-called design orienting scenarios (DOSs) intended to inspire today's designers to create sustainable innovations that might help reach these future scenarios:

1   *Easy clothing care* – high technology home clothes-cleaning equipment, for example a machine that washes, dry-cleans and dries with microwaves, makes clothing care easy and convenient

2   *Soft clothing care* – people air, wash or dry clean their clothes at home as a daily activity using 'soft', environmentally friendly techniques

3   *Clothes leasing centres* – clothes are rented or loaned from service providers who also wash, clean, iron and repair them

4   *My clothes, my eternal friends* – people own a limited wardrobe of high-quality, largely made-to-measure, clothes kept clean and repaired by a laundry service

5   *Collective clothing care* – high-quality clothes are shared and exchanged in a local clothing centre, where they may also be cleaned.

Further workshops generated specific proposals for possible product and service innovations (e.g. 'smart' fabrics that repel and detect dirt, a combined launderette and café) that could help in reaching the future desired situation.

The scenarios and proposals were then evaluated in three ways. First, according to their potential for reducing environmental impacts by up to 95%; secondly, for their economic effects and the business opportunities they offered; and thirdly, for their acceptability to consumers.

I'll now look in more detail at two of the scenarios that were more positively evaluated:

Soft clothing care

In this scenario of the future in 2050, you continuously care for your clothes a little each day. When you undress, you inspect the clothes to decide what to do with each item, cleaning them if required using softer, more environmentally friendly cleaning techniques and equipment. Design proposals for soft clothing care include a wardrobe with a compartment to air, deodorise and refresh clothes overnight and washing pools to soak and slow clean with enzymes, again overnight (Figure 76).

Environmental assessment

Traditional washing techniques are only used when clothes are very dirty. Alternative softer washing techniques are used to freshen up clothes, resulting in significant energy and water savings. Clothes last longer because of the soft nature of the cleaning process and approximately 10% less clothes are bought. The environmental savings in Soft Care are relatively small compared to the other scenarios because the amount of new clothes bought is not significantly reduced. Therefore, this scenario could be combined with other strategies to reduce the amount of clothes bought and encourage the sharing of washing equipment.

Consumer acceptance

Some consumers evaluated this scenario positively, especially given the incremental changes involved and a reduction in the quantity of clothes needed. However, there was scepticism about the time required for

Figure 76   Soft clothing-care scenario. (a) You undress at night and put your clothes in various soft-cleaning facilities. (b) You hang jacket and trousers in the 'climatised wardrobe' with, if necessary, a stain remover patch on the cuffs. (c) You put shirt and underwear in the cleaning pool with the amounts of water and enzyme cleaner indicated by a dirt detector.
Source: adapted from Maschi, in Young and Vergragt, 2000, pp. 10–11

clothing care by those not currently involved in this activity as well as the addition of new devices in the household.

Clothes leasing centres

In this future scenario, clothes are leased from professional Clothes Leasing Centres (Figure 77) that take care of washing, cleaning, ironing, repair... People would not own clothes anymore, except some pieces for sentimental reasons. They are free from any maintenance concerns: there are no laundry appliances at home, and no personal wardrobe (except for underwear and other intimate garments, some of which might be disposable).

Figure 77 Clothes-leasing centre scenario. Customers rent clothes from the centre and get them cleaned and repaired there. Source: Knot and van der Wel, 2001, p. 7

Various types of clothing supply and care services take the place of clothes shops. They are equipped with large-scale clothing care systems allowing much more eco-efficient maintenance processes than domestic ones. Furthermore, individual pieces of clothing are used more intensively: this decreases the quantity of clothes to be produced. At the same time, leasing offers a wide variety of choice and allows styles to change without extending personal wardrobe and costs.

Environmental assessment

A clothes-leasing system with high-quality clothes that are intensively used results in a 35%–95% reduction in material usage, water usage, pesticides and textile waste and a 20%–50% reduction in energy. However, if disposable underwear is used, material usage and textile waste will increase. The Clothes Leasing Centre is combined with a professional laundry service that uses 50% less detergents, water and energy as households use for the same amount of laundry. However, additional transport needed to collect and deliver laundry and the use of clothes driers pose additional environmental burdens.

Consumer acceptance

This scenario was perceived positively by the consumer focus groups who evaluated it. The consumers especially appreciated services like professional clothes washing, repair and recycling as giving increased quality of life, more comfort and time saving.

Caring for clothes outside the home was seen as a positive example of the current trend towards a service society. However, it was difficult to communicate the idea of not only outsourcing clothing-care activities but also outsourcing the ownership of clothes. Some consumers appreciated that they could have more variety with leased or rented clothes, while those who use clothes as a way to express themselves had most reservations over renting clothes. So, consumer acceptance could be further increased for the outsourcing scenario by a mixed system: consumers could if they wished use the total clothing-care service, but they could just take advantage of the clothing-care services while still owning all or most of their clothes.

The five scenarios for sustainable clothing care, plus scenarios for the future of shelter and of food, are given in detail in the SusHouse material on the T307 DVD. You may wish to view (or review) this material at the end of the section, referring to any instructions on using SusHouse provided separately.

I suggest that you start by looking at the hypertext for the two clothing care scenarios mentioned above, and then read the 'storyboard' in the Research reports section, describing what life might be like in 2050 if these scenarios happened. If you wish, you can then explore other scenarios and storyboards on clothing, shelter (heating, lighting and cooling) and food (shopping, cooking and eating).

Exercise 9   Sustainable innovation scenarios

Look at one or more of the clothing care scenarios and read the associated storyboard(s). Consider:

(a) whether you would like to live in such a future

(b) what changes might make it more acceptable to you

(b) what technical and/or social innovations could help to get from now to that future?

You could repeat the exercise for shelter or food scenarios, either individually or as a small group discussion.

In this section, I've shown that (all other things being equal) to achieve the major reductions in energy/resource consumption and emissions required for global sustainability will require long-term system level changes. That's strategy 4 (sustainable innovation) in the design for environment hierarchy introduced at the beginning of Section 7. Some of the ideas might appear improbable, undesirable or even like science fiction. Nevertheless, a few far-sighted businesses such as Philips with its 'third horizon' thinking, and governments in projects such as Sustainable Technology Development and SusHouse, are exploring such radical changes. Radical system level or configurational socio-technical innovations clearly pose major issues of cultural, social, economic and political acceptability. But if they are not explored in possible future scenarios, there will not be the option to adopt such innovations, if and when required, to achieve the 90% or greater reductions in resource consumption and emissions for long-term environmental sustainability.

9.4   Conclusion: innovation is not enough

In this block, I've looked at new product development, ranging from minor design improvements to radical technical innovations, and design for the environment, ranging from single issue green product design to systems-level sustainable innovation.

Of course, it's not enough to develop a new product, ecodesign, sustainable design or innovation. These innovations have to be introduced, accepted and adopted by individuals or organisations to have any commercial, social or environmental effects. As they diffuse, new products and systems are usually improved and so evolve.

For example, the scenarios for sustainable clothing care involve innovations in socio-technical systems, new infrastructure and changes to the economy and values of a consumer society in which designing and making clothes is a global industry, fashion is an important element of culture, and buying clothes provides pleasure for many people. The social and cultural changes that may be required to move towards sustainable clothing care are therefore less likely, at least in the short term, than technical and design changes that increase the 'eco-efficiency' of clothes care systems. The same is true of other products and systems that consume large amounts of energy and resources, such as electricity supply, transport and housing.

The diffusion of products and innovations and the involvement of users in the evolution of sustainable products and systems, and the question of whether even sustainable innovation will be enough to reach sustainability, is the subject of later blocks this course.

Key points of Section 9

- Reducing the impacts of individual products by ecodesign will not be enough to reduce energy and resource consumption by some 90% required to deal with the environmental problems posed by increasing global levels of production and consumption up to 2050 and beyond. The challenge has led to the concepts of sustainable design and sustainable innovation.

- Sustainable design can mean taking ecodesign to its limits, for example through Datschefski's five principles of a sustainable product. Alternatively, sustainable design means devising alternative environmentally optimal technical means for providing the essential function of a product.

- Philips sees sustainability as comprising social, economic and environmental responsibilities. In pursuit of its strategy of sustainable development, the company is attempting to embed ecodesign and sustainable design throughout its organisation, and is moving towards sustainable innovation via new sustainable business initiatives in the developing world.

- Sustainable innovation involves moving from the design of individual products to the design of whole systems. It can involve as new mixes of products and services, new patterns of ownership, or shared/communal use of products. It might involve replacing physical products with a 'dematerialised' service or even questioning the extent to which a product or service is really necessary.

- Technical 'eco-efficiency' approaches to environmental sustainability are more acceptable and therefore more likely in the short and medium term than attempts to introduce radical, socio-technical sustainable innovations.

- Some far-sighted businesses and governments are studying long-term future ideas and scenarios involving sustainable innovation. This is partly to ensure long-term profitability or economic survival and partly to avoid people and organisations being forced to adapt in less desirable ways to the challenges of environmental sustainability.

Answers to self-assessment questions

SAQ 1

In 2000, Black & Decker launched the Mouse sander (Figure 3a), a novel form of detail sander for the do-it yourself market. It was designed to have some of the qualities of a computer mouse – its small size to fit in the hand and the ease with which it moves across a surface – giving it the control to reach tight corners.

(a) What type of new product is the Mouse sander for Black & Decker?

(b) What type of innovation does the Mouse represent for the world?

(c) A new model Mouse with gel grips at the top and sides for greater comfort in use was launched in 2004. What type of change does this represent?

(a) the Mouse was an addition to Black & Decker's sander product line (that also includes conventional abrasive sheet and belt sanders).

(b) it is an architectural innovation: a novel configuration of existing components (motor, vibrator unit, abrasive sheets, and so on)

(c) the Mouse with gel grips is an improvement to an existing product.

SAQ 2

Figure 4 shows a few of the over 1000 products chosen for the Design Council's Millennium Products programme. These were selected for being innovative in one or more aspects, including: challenging existing ideas, solving a key problem, opening up a new market, applying existing or new technology, being environmentally responsible. So far as you are able, classify each according to the main type of new product or innovation it represents.

(a) Adaptive spectacles. A new-to-the-world product and modular innovation.

(b) Hi-fi loudspeaker. An addition to an existing product line and architectural innovation.

(c) Electric string instruments. A new product line and modular innovation.

(d) Milk chocolate bar. A new product line and incremental innovation.

(e) Self-powered lantern. An addition to an existing product line and modular innovation.

(f) Computer and voice synthesiser. A new-to-the-world product and modular innovation.

(g) Solar hot water system. A new product line and architectural innovation.

SAQ 3

Give two recent examples each of sustaining and disruptive innovations.

1   Sustaining

(a) single-use film cameras

(b) hi-fi super audio CDs (SA-CDs) and compatible music players.

2   Disruptive

(a) digital cameras, storage media, software, and printers

(b) internet music stores and associated computer software and music players, for example Apple iTunes and the iPod.

SAQ 4

What organisational structure would you choose for (a) the design of an innovative consumer product and (b) a large-scale engineering project involving technical innovation? Give reasons for your choice.

(a) For an innovative product design project, such as the development of a novel item of consumer electronics, a pure project organisation should offer the creative and multidisciplinary benefits of a dedicated team and aid rapid product development.

(b) For a large-scale engineering project involving technical innovation, for example the development of a hybrid car or fast train, a strong matrix organisation under a 'heavyweight' project manager would offer many of the benefits of a project team, but with access to the specialist expertise and resources of the team members' functional departments.

SAQ 5

Draw a table to show how the main phases and checkpoints of Electrolux's integrated product development process (Figure 29b) and Philips' product creation process (Figure 20) compare to Pugh's design process model and Cooper's stage-gate model outlined in Section 2 of this block.

How do the idealised models, and the use of NPD teams discussed in Section 3, compare with recommended practice at Electrolux and Philips?

Table 9

Electrolux IPDP	Philips PCP	Design process model	Stage-gate model
project specification CP00/CP0	0 feasibility 1 definition	market specification	discovery/gate 1 stage 1: scoping/ gate 2 stage 2: business case/gate 3
project industrialisation CP1/CP2/CP3	2 system design 3 engineering 4 integration and test	concept design (embodiment design) detail design	stage 3: development/ gate 4 stage 4: testing/gate 5
production feedback	5 field monitoring	manufacture sell	stage 5: launch post-launch review

Table 9 shows that the flow of Electrolux's IPDP and Philips' PCP follows the design process and stage-gate models quite closely – practice follows theory. There are, however, some differences in the order in which specific activities are supposed to be undertaken, to suit the practices of each organisation. Electrolux and Philips also use cross-functional team approaches to NPD, although the organisational structure (for example a pure project, a strong matrix or a weak matrix) differs from project to project.

SAQ 6

What competitive strategy did Flymo pursue to compete in the garden products market with the Garden Vac? What response did Black & Decker adopt after Flymo had successfully launched the Garden Vac?

The Garden Vac was the result of Flymo pursuing a 'first-to-market' strategy. This led to the development of an invention, originally created outside the company, into an innovative new-to-the-world product. Note Flymo's use of ergonomic and industrial design expertise to ensure the product was easy to use, attractive and economic to manufacture.

Flymo then maintained its market position by following the original innovation with incremental improvements such as the Garden Vac Plus with an integral shredder based on the nylon line cutters used in its garden strimmer products.

Black & Decker, who failed to gain the licence to develop the Garden Vac, responded to its successful market launch and sales with a 'follow-the-leader' strategy. Black & Decker's product was based on re-engineering an existing US 'blowervac' product, as it could not copy Flymo's patented Garden Vac technology.

SAQ 7

Using Porter's competitive strategies, what do technical innovation and product design offer in helping a company to gain a competitive advantage? Give one or more examples to illustrate your answer.

Both technical innovation and product design can help companies gain competitive advantage. They can (a) reduce production costs by process innovation and design for economic manufacture (a lower-cost strategy). They can (b) increase product performance, quality and reliability and enable a company to offer unique products or special design features through product and/or process innovations and new designs (a differentiation strategy).

Elements of both these approaches are present in the Garden Groom and Garden Vac cases. Both were innovative products designed for economic manufacture, optimum technical performance, attractive visual appearance, and good ergonomics.

SAQ 8

What are the links between the project, organisational and strategic levels of NPD introduced in Part 1

The *strategic* level attempts to plan NPD project(s) that supports the strategy of an individual or company.

The *organisational* level attempts to establish an appropriate structure (for example a strong matrix) for organising and managing an individual NPD project.

The *project* level establishes a process (for example a stage-gate process) for undertaking an individual NPD project.

SAQ 9

Different EU and EC directives and regulations aim to reduce environmental impacts at different parts of a product's life cycle: from materials supply, through manufacture and use, to end-of-life recycling or disposal.

(a) Match the EU and EC directives in Box 4 to the most relevant parts of the product's life cycle.

(b) Which directives should be addressed during NPD?

(c) Which directives are examples of 'extended producer responsibility'?

(a) Materials: RoSH; Batteries; IPP.

Manufacture: EMAS; RoSH; IPP.

Use: energy label; EuP; IPP.

End of life: Packaging; EMAS; ELVD; WEEE, Batteries; IPP.

(b) All of the above could, and should, be addressed during the NPD process.

(c) ELVD; WEEE.

SAQ 10

What were the main external and internal drivers that led Black & Decker to establish and undertake a design for the environment programme? Look back at the list of environmental drivers at the beginning of Section 6, the above case study and Figure 37.

1   External drivers

   (a) environmental legislation and regulation, for example EU hazardous substances and packaging directives EMAS and ISO 14001

   (b) pressure from retailer customers, for example B&Q

   (c) introduction of green products by competitors, for example Electrolux, Bosch

   (d) innovations in technology, for example batteries.

2   Internal drivers

   (a) cost savings, for example design for ease of assembly and disassembly

   (b) corporate social responsibility.

SAQ 11

(a) What led Philips to adopt a sustainability policy?

(b) What is Philips' strategy for growth within its sustainability policy?

(a) Philips has been concerned with social issues since the late nineteenth century and with environmental issues since at least the 1970s. Philips considers that bringing together its social, economic and environmental responsibilities into a sustainability policy driven by a corporate sustainability office is the best way to ensure its long-term profitability, survival and growth.

(b) Philips aims to grow from a €30 to a €50 billion business. Its strategy for doing this is to provide the most technically advanced, user-friendly products for Western markets, to develop low-cost versions of existing products and to create new business initiatives for the newly industrialised and developing world. As part of Philips' sustainability policy, this includes trying to provide products affordable and relevant to the four billion people at the bottom of the economic pyramid.

SAQ 12

(a) How does Philips attempt to meet its environmental responsibilities within its sustainability policy?

(b) How is the company embedding ecodesign into the product creation process?

(a) Philips bases its environmental policy on programmes called EcoVision that set environmental improvement targets for the product divisions and businesses to reach in both their manufacturing processes and product design.

(b) Philips has developed a simple checklist approach to ecodesign based on five green focal areas for divisions that are still developing their environmental awareness and skills. One drawback is that focusing on just one or two focal areas can lead to a sub-optimal design from an environmental viewpoint. So designers who wish to adopt a more systematic ecodesign approach are encouraged first to take products apart and then use life-cycle assessment software to assess the impacts of all the product components and so help decide the optimal environmental improvements. Under the triple bottom line sustainability policy, these environmental improvements have to be assessed to see if they are economically viable and, perhaps, if they are socially useful.

SAQ 13

Why does Philips believe it can grow economically while still being socially and environmentally sustainable?

The company seems to have shifted its ground from arguing it's possible to simultaneously meet its three responsibilities to stating that it's sometimes necessary to balance the 'sometimes-competing' demands of people, profit and planet. Inevitably, in such a big organisation, there are different views on how to achieve this balance.

The official view appears to be that technology will allow socially and environmentally sustainable economic growth to continue, perhaps until everyone in India and China has a Western quality of life. Others in the company argue that such unfettered growth isn't sustainable and that new patterns of production and consumption will have to emerge.

References and further reading

Ansoff, H. I. and Stewart, J. (1967) Strategies for technology-based business, *Harvard Business Review*, November–December, pp. 71–83.

Boisot, M. and von Stamm, B. (1996) Toward a contingency theory of the design process: the case of Eurostar, in vol. 1 of *Proceedings of the 8th International Forum on Design Management Research and Education*, Barcelona, November.

Boothroyd, G., Dewhurst, P. and Knight, W. (2002) *Product Design for Manufacture and Assembly*, 2nd edn, New York, Marcel Dekker.

Booz-Allen and Hamilton (1982) *New Product Management for the 1980s*, New York, Booz-Allen and Hamilton Inc.

Boyle, G. and Harper, P. (eds) (1976) *Radical Technology*, London, Wildwood House.

Brezet, H. (1997) Dynamics in ecodesign practice, *UNEP Industry and Environment*, Special issue on Product Development and the Environment, vol. 20, nos 1–2, January-June, pp. 21–24.

Brezet, H. and van Hemel, C. (1997) *Ecodesign. A Promising Approach to Sustainable Production and Consumption*, Paris, United Nations Environment Programme.

Broers, A. (2005) *The triumph of technology*, Reith Lectures 2005, BBC Radio 4, 6 April–4 May, http://www.bbc.co.uk/radio4/reith2005 (accessed 19.7.05)

BSI (1989, 1997) *BS 7000: Design management systems: Part 2. Guide to the design of manufactured products*, London, British Standards Institution.

Caluwe, N. de (2004) Business benefits from applied ecodesign, *IEEE Transactions on Electronics Packaging Manufacturing*, vol. 27, no. 4, October, pp. 215–220.

Chang, H.-T. and Chen, J. L. (2003) Eco-Innovative examples for 40 TRIZ inventive principles, http://www.triz-journal/archives/2003/08a/01.pdf (accessed 20.4.05)

Chick, A. (1997) The 'Freeplay' radio, *Journal of Sustainable Product Design*, Issue 1, April, pp. 53–56.

Christensen, C. M. (2003) *The Innovator's Dilemma: The Revolutionary Book that Will Change the Way you Do Business*, New York, HarperBusiness Essentials.

Cooper, R. G. (2001) *Winning at New Products*, 3rd edn, Cambridge, MA, Perseus Publishing.

Corbett, J. (1991) *Design for Manufacture: Strategies, Principles and Techniques*, Wokingham, Addison Wesley.

Datschefski, E. (1999) Progress towards sustainable design in the white goods sector, *Journal of Sustainable Product Design*, July, pp. 43–52.

Datschefski, E. (2001) *The Total Beauty of Sustainable Products*, Switzerland, RotoVision.

DEFRA (2005) *Securing the Future. The UK Government Sustainable Development Strategy*, CM6467, Department of Environment, Food and Rural Affairs, March, London, The Stationery Office.

DEFRA (2005) A comparison of washing up by hand with a domestic dishwasher, BNW16, Market Transformation Programme, http://www.mtprog.com/Briefing Notes (accessed 1.4.05)

Design Council (2000) *Here's to the Best of British. 1,012 Millennium Products*, London, The Design Council.

Electrolux (2005) Environmental strategy and policy, http://www.electrolux.com/node455.asp (accessed 4.8.05)

Elliott, D. (1997) *Energy, Society and Environment*, London, Routledge.

ENDS (1996) Building the 'green' factor into product development, *The ENDS Report*, No. 260 (September), pp. 23–25.

Envirowise (2001) *Cleaner product design; examples from industry*, Didcot, Envirowise, September. http://www.envirowise.gov.uk (accessed 1.2.05)

EPA (2002) Fact sheet: mercury in compact fluorescent lamps, US Environmental Protection Agency, http://www.nema.org/lamprecycle/epafactsheet-cfl.pdf (accessed 15.4.04)

Fleck, J. (1994) Learning by trying. The importance of configurational technology, *Research Policy*, 23, pp. 637–652.

Floyd, J. (2001) EDPD4 *Major project report: Electric doughnut kinetic charger*, London, South Bank University, May/June.

Foster, R. N. (1988) *Innovation: The Attacker's Advantage*, New York, Summit Books.

Fowles, M. (2004) The inception of technological innovations, Powerpoint presentation, Department of Design and Innovation, Faculty of Technology, Milton Keynes, The Open University, April.

Freeman, C. (1982) *The Economics of Industrial Innovation*, 2nd edn, London, Frances Pinter.

Green, K. and Vergracht, P. (2002) Towards sustainable households: a methodology for developing sustainable technological and social innovations, *Futures*, vol. 34, no. 5, June, pp. 381–400.

Greenwood, T. (2004) *A Guide to Environmentally Sustainable Product Design*, http://www.espdesign.org (accessed 20.1.05)

Henderson, R. M. and Clark, K. B. (1990) Architectural innovation: the reconfiguration of existing product technologies and the failure of established firms, *Administrative Science Quarterly*, vol. 35, no. 1, March, pp. 9–30.

HM Treasury (2005) *Energy efficiency innovation review: summary report*, London, HMSO, December

Hollins, G. and Hollins, B. (1991) *Total Design. Managing the Design Process in the Service Sector*, London, Pitman.

Hoover (1990) *The Hoover Environmental Mission*, Hoover Ltd.

IDSA (Industrial Designers Society of America) (2001) *Design Secrets: Products*, Gloucester, MA, Rockport Publishers.

ISO (2002) *Environmental management – Integrating environmental aspects into product design and development* (ISO/TR 14062), Geneva, International Standards Organisation.

Jerrard, R., Hands, D. and Ingram, J. (2002) Electrolux. The management of complexity in a large organisation, in Jerrard, R. et al (eds), *Design Management Case Studies*, London and New York, Routledge, pp. 8–20.

Jolly, A. (2003) *Innovation: Harnessing Creativity for Business Growth*, London, Kogan Page.

Jones, T. (1997) *New Product Development. An introduction to a Multi-functional Process*, Oxford, Butterworth-Heinemann.

Kirby, N. and Gabbitas, B. (1996) Fresh air in packaging design, *Co-design*, 05/06, pp. 92–96.

Knot, M. and van der Wel, M. (2001) Creativity for sustainable development: the SusHouse approach, illustrated for clothing care, *Journal of Design Research*, Issue 2, http://jdr.tudelft.nl/articles/ (accessed 1.4.05)

Kotler, P. (1988) *Marketing Management: Analysis, Planning, Implementation and Control*, 6th edn, Englewood Cliffs, Prentice Hall.

Lawson, B. (1990) *How Designers Think*, 2nd edn, London, Butterworth Architecture.

Lees, N. (2003) Mattel taps its creative juices with the power of Platypus, *KidScreen Magazine*, 1 March, p. 57, http://www.kidscreen.com/articles/magazine/20030301/platypus.html (accessed 21.7.05)

Lewis, H., Gertsakis, J., Grant, T., Morelli, N. and Sweatman, A. (2001) *Design + Environment: A Global Guide to Designing Greener Goods*, Sheffield, Greenleaf.

Meadows, D.H. (1974) *The Limits to Growth: a report for the Club of Rome's project on the predicament of mankind*, London, Pan Books.

Mildenberger, U. and Khare, A. (2000) Planning for an environment-friendly car, *Technovation*, vol. 20, pp. 205–214.

Muller, G. (2004) The Product Creation Process, Eindhoven, The Netherlands, Embedded Systems Institute, August, http://www.extra.research.philips.com/natlab/sysarch/ (accessed 25.7.05)

Myerson, J. (2001) *IDEO: Masters of Innovation*, London, Laurence King.

Nokia (2003) *Environmental Report 2002*, http://www.nokia.com (accessed 25.2.05)

Nokia (2005) *Integrated Product Policy Pilot Project*, Nokia Corporation, January, http://europa.eu.int/comm/environment/ipp/pdf/impact_nokia.pdf (accessed 3.3.05)

Open University (1996) T302 *Innovation: design, environment and strategy*, Block 4 'Innovative product development', Milton Keynes, The Open University.

Open University (1999a) T302 *Innovation: design, environment and strategy*, Block 4 'Case studies', 2nd edn, Milton Keynes, The Open University.

Open University (1999b) T302 *Innovation: design, environment and strategy*, Video Guide for Block 4, 'Green product development – the Hoover New Wave', in T302 TV, Video and Audio Guides, 2nd edn, Milton Keynes, The Open University, pp. 24–46.

Open University (2001a) T840 *The strategic management of technology*, Block 2 'Patterns of innovation and improvement', Milton Keynes, The Open University.

Open University (2001b) T173 *Engineering the future*, Block 2 'Engineering by design', Milton Keynes, The Open University.

Open University (2003) T206 *Power for a Sustainable Future*, Block 3, Chapter 2 'Sustainable road transport techniques', Milton Keynes, The Open University, pp. 29–67.

Open University (2004a) T211 *Design and designing*, Block 1 'An introduction to design and designing', Milton Keynes, The Open University.

Open University (2004b) T211 *Design and designing*, Block 2 'User requirements and the design brief', Milton Keynes, The Open University.

Open University (2004c) T211 *Design and designing*, Block 5 'Detail design and manufacture', Milton Keynes, The Open University.

Office of Technology Assessment, of Congress of the United States (2005) *Green Products by Design: Choices for a Cleaner Environment*, Honolulu, HI, University Press of the Pacific.

PA Consulting Group (1991) *Environmental labelling of washing machines. A pilot study for the DTI/DOE*, Royston, UK, PA Consulting Group.

Pahl, G. and Beitz, W. (1984) *Engineering Design* (2nd edn), 1996, London, Springer.

Papanek, V. (1971) *Design for the Real World*, 2nd edn 1984, London, Thames and Hudson.

Philips (c. 1996) *The Environmental opportunity. Ecodesign*, Eindhoven, The Netherlands, Philips Corporate Environmental and Energy Office.

Philips (2005) *Sustainability Report 2004*, Royal Philips Electronics, February, http://www.philips.com/about/sustainability, (accessed 4.4.05)

Philips (2006) Creating *Value. Sustainability Report 2005*, Royal Philips Electronics http://www.philips.com/about/sustainability (accessed 19.03.06)

Porter, M. E. (1990) *The Competitive Advantage of Nations*, London and Basingstoke, Macmillan.

Potter, S. (1986) *On the Right Lines?*, London, Frances Pinter.

Potter, S. (1999) Managing the design of an innovative green transport project, *The Design Journal*, vol. 2, issue 3, pp. 51–60.

Pugh, S. (1998) *Total Design. Integrated Methods for Successful Product Engineering*, 2nd edn, Wokingham, Addison Wesley.

Rothwell, R. (1992) Successful industrial innovation: critical factors for the 1990s, *R&D Management*, vol. 22, no. 3, pp. 221–239.

Roy, R. (1997) Design for environment in practice – development of the Hoover New Wave washing machine range, *Journal of Sustainable Product Design*, Issue 1, April, pp. 36–43.

Roy, R. (1999) Designing and marketing greener products. The Hoover case, in Charter, M. and Polonsky, J. (eds) *Greener Marketing. A Global Perspective on Greener Marketing Practice*, Sheffield, Greenleaf, pp. 126–142.

Ryan, C. (2004) *Digital eco-sense: sustainability and ICT – a new terrain for innovation*, Victoria, Australia, Lab.3000, http://www.lab.3000.com.au (accessed 19.3.06)

Schmidheiney, S. (1992) *Changing Course: A Global Business Perspective on Development and the Environment*, Boston, MA, MIT Press.

Shetty, D. (2002) *Design for Product Success*, Dearborn, MI, Society for Manufacturing Engineers.

Sweatman, A. and Gertsakis, J. (1996) Eco-kettle: keep the kettle boiling, *Co-design* 05/06, pp. 97–99.

Thompson, P. and Sherwin, C. (2001) 'Awareness'. Sustainability by industrial design, in Charter, M. and Tischner, U., *Sustainable Solutions. Developing Products and Services for the Future*, Sheffield, Greenleaf, pp. 349–363.

Thompson, R. (2004) A life by design, *Harvard Business School Alumni Bulletin*, December, http://www.alumni.hbs.edu/bulletin/2004/december/index.html (accessed 19.7.05)

Thurston, D. L. (1994) Environmental design trade-offs, *Journal of Engineering Design*, vol. 5, no. 1, pp. 25–36.

Ulrich, K.T. and Eppinger, S. D. (2000) *Product Design and Development*, 2nd edn, New York, McGraw-Hill.

UNEP (1999) *Global environmental outlook 2000. UNEP's Millennium report on the environment*, Nairobi, United Nations Environment Programme, London, Earthscan.

Usher, A. P. (1954) *A History of Mechanical Inventions* (rev. edn), Cambridge MA, Harvard University Press.

V & A (March, 2005) *International Arts and Crafts*, Exhibition guide, London, Victoria and Albert Museum.

VDI 2221 (1987) *Systematic Approach to the Design of Technical Systems and Products*, Dusseldorf, VDI-Verlag GmbH.

von Stamm, B. and Boisot, M. (1996) Integrating design and organisation, Report to the Design Council, London.

von Weizsäcker, E., Lovins, A. B. and Lovins, L. H. (1997) *Factor Four. Doubling Wealth – Halving Resource Use*, London, Earthscan.

Ward, J. (2002) In trim, *New Design*, September/October, pp. 72–73.

Weaver, P. M. et al (2000) *Sustainable Technology Development*, Sheffield, Greenleaf.

Weisberg. R. W. (1993) *Creativity. Beyond the Myth of Genius*, New York, W. H. Freeman.

Wenzel, H., Hauschild, M. and Alting, L. (1997) *Environmental Assessment of Products, Volume 1: Methodology, Tools and Studies in Product Development*, London, Chapman and Hall.

Winstanley, D. and Francis, A. (1988) Fast forward for design managers, *Engineering*, March, pp. 133–135.

World Commission on Environment and Development (1987) *Our Common Future* (Brundtland report), Oxford, Oxford University Press.

Zacharias, C. (2004) Project Platypus: Mattel's unconventional toy development process (ICFIA Business School Case Development Centre, Hyderabad, India.), Case 404–005–1, Cranfield, UK, European Case Clearing House.

Acknowledgements

Grateful acknowledgement is made to the following sources for permission to reproduce material within this book.

Every effort has been made to contact copyright holders. If any have been inadvertently overlooked the publishers will be pleased to make the necessary arrangements at the first opportunity.

Text

Box 2: Adapted from Cooper R. G. (2001), 'Accelerating the Process from Idea to Launch', *Winning at New Products*, Perseus Books.

Pages 27–29: Adapted from Ward, J. 'In trim', *New Design,* September/October 2002, New Design Magazine.

Pages 38–43: Adapted from Jones, J. (1997) *New Product Development: an Introduction to Multi-Functional Process.* 1st edn., pp. 52–63. Copyright © 1997, with permission from Elsevier.

Pages 116–118: Brezet, H. and Von Hemel, C. (1997) 'Exhibit 3.31 MET Matrix applied to the Veromatic professional Coffee Machine Ecodesign: A Promising Approach to Sustainable Production and Consumption, United National Environment Programme.

Tables

Table 1: Ulrich K. and Eppinger S. (2000) *Product Design and Development*, The McGraw-Hill Companies. Copyright © 2000, 1995 by the McGraw-Hill Companies, Inc. All rights reserved. Reproduced with permission.

Table 3: Wenzel, H. et al, (1997) *Environmental Assessment of Products, Volume 1: Methodology, Tools, and Studies in Product Development,* Chapman and Hall. With kind permission of Springer Science and Business Media.

Tables 5 and 7: Brezet, H. and Von Hemel, C. (1997) 'Exhibit 3.31 MET Matrix applied to the Veromatic professional Coffee Machine Ecodesign: A Promising Approach to Sustainable Production and Consumption, United National Environment Programme.

Figures

Figure 1: Kotler, P. *Marketing Management: Analysis, Planning, Implementation and Control*, 6th Edition © 1988. Reprinted by permission of Pearson Education, Inc., Upper Saddle River, N. J. Prentice Hall.

Figure 3: © Copyright Black and Decker, Inc. 2004, reproduced with permission.

Figure 4: (a) Courtesy of Adaptive Eyecare Ltd; (b) Courtesy of B&W Group; (c) Courtesy of Bridge Musical Instruments; (d) Copyright © The Day Chocolate Company; (e) Courtesy of Freeplay; (f) Courtesy of Cambridge Adaptive Communications; (g) Courtesy of Thermomax (GB) Ltd.

Figures 6 and 7: Courtesy of JCB.

Figure 9: (a) Adapted from Pugh, S. (1991) *Total Design*, Addison Wesley Longman; (c) Extract from BS7000: 1989, BSI.

Figure 10: Courtesy of DCA Design International Ltd.

Figure 11: Floyd, J. (2001) *EDPD4 Major project report: Electric doughnut kinetic charger*, South Bank University. © Copyright 2001 Justin Floyd.

Figure 12: Courtesy of Porta-Charge Ltd.

Figure 14: Cooper R. G. (2001), 'Accelerating the Process from Idea to Launch', *Winning at New Products*, Perseus Books.

Figures 15 and 16: Courtesy of Electrolux.

Figure 17: Courtesy of Umbrolly.

Figure 19: Winstanley, D. and Francis, A. 'Fast forward for design managers', *Engineering*, March 1988.

Figure 20: Muller, G. (2004) 'The Product Creation Process', Embedded Systems Institute, The Netherlands.

Figure 21: Courtesy of JCB.

Figure 22: Ulrich K. and Eppinger S. (2000) *Product Design and Development*, The McGraw-Hill Companies. Copyright © 2000, 1995 by the McGraw-Hill Companies, Inc. All rights reserved. Reproduced with permission.

Figure 26: Courtesy of Eurostar.

Figure 27: Boisot, M. and von Stamm, B. 'Toward a contingency theory of the design process: the case of Eurostar', *Proceedings of the 8th International Forum on Design and Management Research and Education*, November 1996, Barcelona.

Figure 29: Jerrard R., Hands D. and Ingram J. (2002) 'Electrolux. The management of complexity in a large organisation', *Design Management Case Studies*, Routledge, Taylor & Francis.

Figure 30: Courtesy of Dyson plc.

Figure 31: Courtesy of Electrolux.

Figure 33: Courtesy of Kodak.

Figure 34: Fridge photo © Alamy Images.

Figure 35: Electrolux (2005) Environmental strategy and policy, http://electrolux.com.

Figure 36: Courtesy of weeeman.org.

Figure 37: Courtesy of Envirowise.

Figure 40: Courtesy of Remarkable Ltd.

Figure 41: (a) Trannon Ltd.; (b) Courtesy of Baxi Potterton; (c) © Foxfibre from 'The Total Beauty of Sustainable Products' by Edwin Datschefski, published by RotoVision.

Figure 45: (a) Courtesy of Blue Line.

Figures 46 and 47a: Sweatman, A. and Gertsakis, J. 'Eco-kettle: keep the kettle boiling', *Co-Design*, 05/06, 1996. www.co-design.co.uk

Figure 48: Courtesy of Bang & Olufsen.

Figures 49 and 57: Wenzel, H. et al, (1997) *Environmental Assessment of Products, Volume 1: Methodology, Tools, and Studies in Product Development*, Chapman and Hall. With kind permission of Springer Science and Business Media.

Figure 50b: Courtesy of Veromatic International BV.

Figure 51: Brezet, H. and Von Hemel, C. (1997) 'Exhibit 3.31 MET Matrix applied to the Veromatic professional Coffee Machine Ecodesign: A Promising Approach to Sustainable Production and Consumption, United National Environment Programme.

Figure 53: Adapted from Thurston, D. L. 'Environmental design trade-offs', *Journal of Engineering Design*, Vol. 5 No.1, 1994. Taylor & Francis.

Figure 54: (a) With permission from Cranfield University; (b) Courtesy of DaimlerChrysler.

Figure 56: Department for Transport, 'Fuel Economy Ford Fiesta, www.dft.gov.uk. Crown © Copyright. Crown copyright material is reproduced under Class Licence Number C01W0000065, with the permission of the Controller of HMSO and the Queen's Printer for Scotland.

Figures 58, 61 and 63 Hoover European Appliance Group.

Figure 62: © European Commission.

Figure 67b: Chick, A. 'The Freeplay radio', *Journal of Sustainable Design*, No. 1 April 1997, The Centre of Sustainable Design.

Figure 68: The Freeplay Group.

Figures 69, 71–73: Philips (2005) *Sustainability Report 2004*, http://www.philips.com

Figure 70: Philips (c.1996) *The Environmental Opportunity. Ecodesign*, Philips Corporate Environmental and Energy Office.

Figure 75a: Courtesy of Sanyo; (b) Chang, H.T. and Chen, J. L. 'Eco-Innovative examples for 40 TRIZ inventive principles', *Triz Journal*, August 2003, http://www.triz-journal.com/archives/2003/08/a/01.pdf

Figure 76: Maschi, S. in Young, C. W. and Vergragt, P. (eds) (2000) *Strategies Towards the Sustainable Household (SusHouse) Project: Design Orienting Scenarios*, CROMTEC, Manchester School of Management.

Figure 77: Knot, M. and van der Wel, M. 'Creativity for Sustainable Development', *Journal of Design Research*, Vol. 1 2001, Delft University Press.